Happier Every Day

PAULA MUNIER

Media Lab Books
For inquiries, call 646-838-6637

Copyright 2019 by Paula Munier

Published by Topix Media Lab
14 Wall Street, Suite 4B
New York, NY 10005

Printed in China

ISBN-13: 9781948174077
ISBN-10: 1948174073

For Emma Spencer Boyle and Michelle Fleming,
who taught me how to breathe.

Table of Contents

Introduction

———

"When I was 5 years old, my mother
always told me that happiness was the key to life.
When I went to school, they asked me what I wanted
to be when I grew up. I wrote down 'happy.'
They told me I didn't understand the assignment and I
told them they didn't understand life."
—John Lennon

———

I JUST WANT TO BE HAPPY. How many times have
we heard people say that, and said that ourselves, as if happiness
were a mystery to be solved? My elder son said the same thing
to me when he was suffering through his quarter-life crisis at
25. He asked me how to be happy, and I—winning and wise and
the wonderful earth mother goddess that I believed myself to
be at the time—told him being happy was a byproduct of living
a meaningful life. Everyone needs a reason to get up in the
morning, I told him. The beginning of happiness starts with
greeting the sunrise knowing you matter and that your life
matters—*to you*. Ultimately, you are the source of your
own happiness.

In my own personal happiness myth (we all have them)—
the one I believed in with all my heart—I had learned this the
hard way, just like everyone else. I was lucky, in that I had a

very happy childhood. I was blessed with generous and loving parents who raised me according to an exacting standard of behavior. They expected me to be happy, and so I was. Even though I was always the new kid at school (12 moves in 11 years); even though I was an only child who spent much of my time alone; even though I was expected to be perfect all the time.

But I had my dog and my books and my bike and whatever friends I'd been fortunate enough to make that term. So I was happy.

By the time I was all grown up, I had developed a capacity for happiness that has served me well through the inevitable disappointments and devastations that befall us all sooner or later. For me, that included divorce(s), financial ruin(s), mental illness (first husband), chronic illness (child), broken heart (second husband) and betrayals at home and at work by the people I trusted most.

But I got through it all relatively unscathed and relatively happy, until my youngest child went off to college. When my *raison d'être*—raising my children—was abruptly over.

I was alone again, just like when I was a kid, but this time I had no generous and loving parents waiting at home with open arms. No husband. No kids. And my beloved dog Shakespeare was dying.

I'll just work, I told myself. Work had always saved me before. It would save me again.

And then I got laid off.

Now I really had no reason to get up in the morning.

I was middle-aged and miserable and mourning My Life as I Knew It.

I had to teach myself the art of happiness all over again. This time, I learned it the hard way, *for real*.

Namaste in Bed and Cry

I would always run from unhappiness before. *Move on,* I'd tell myself when the going got gloomy. New people, new places, new experiences never failed to cheer me up. Hit the road and leave my blues in the rearview mirror, that was my modus operandi. And it always worked. Until it didn't.

My salvation came in the form of a practice I'd ridiculed for years: yoga. I went to see Julia Cameron, bestselling author of *The Artist's Way*, to recharge my writing self, since it looked like freelancing was my only option in terms of work now that I'd "aged out" of the corporate world. Cameron was running a writer's workshop at Kripalu, a wellness center in the Berkshires, the kind of woo-woo place where people danced to drums and chanted *om* and said things like "being one with the universe" with a straight face.

But this was Julia Cameron—I'd taken one of her workshops decades before and loved it—so I talked my dear writer friend Susan Reynolds into going with me, to serve as a buffer between me and the crunchies. I rolled my eyes when breakfast was served "in silence" and there was no caffeine or alcohol, and we sat at a table full of people who were there to learn to channel something or other.

But I did go to the yoga classes, only because they were part of the package. That is, free. If you know anything about me, know this: If it's free, I'll try it.

The big surprise? I fell in love with yoga at Kripalu. All of it— the stretching, the breathing and even the *om*-ing.

I came home ready to write and ready to practice yoga. I learned that one of my writer pals had done her yoga teacher training at Kripalu and she recommended that I go to Dragonfly Yoga Studio, run by a Kripalu-trained yoga teacher named Emma Spencer Boyle. Emma taught me how to move. She taught me how to breathe. She taught me how to be.

She taught me how to look inside for the answers I'd always looked to the outside world to provide.

I couldn't get enough yoga. It wasn't enough for me that it worked; I wanted to know why it worked. Why did it feel so good, why did my body feel 10 years younger and my spirit 10 pounds lighter after every class? Why was I so happy, even when my life was falling apart?

My family thought I was losing it. Faced with another long hard New England winter on my own, my kids encouraged me to sign up for yoga teacher training, something for their poor lost mother to do until she regained her sense and sanity.

While it snowed (and snowed and snowed) that winter,

I was as snug as a bug in a yoga rug at Sanctuary Studios, learning the finer points of yoga philosophy and physiology with a class of young and not-so-young yoginis, led by studio owner Michelle Fleming. Michelle's background as a physical therapist and longtime yoga guru allowed her to answer the "whys" of this ancient practice's effectiveness—body, mind and spirit.

Between Emma and Michelle, I learned happiness off the mat was just a deep cleansing breath away from happiness on the mat.

Happier Every Day

Within a year of receiving my yoga teacher certification, my life took many happy turns. My agent, Gina Panettieri, asked me to join her agency, propelling me into a fabulous new career.

My former colleague, Phil Sexton, asked me to write the first of what would become a series of popular books on writing. And most surprising of all, I reconciled with my second husband, Michael.

I know, I know. But as Michelle told me more than once, open your heart (chakra) and love will walk in. If I'd known that love would take the form of my ex-husband, I might never have done it.

And my life would have been far poorer for it.

Which just goes to show happiness is never what we think it

is. I never thought I could be an agent or a writing teacher or a crime novelist (my first mystery, *A Borrowing of Bones*, debuted recently). I certainly never thought I could be with Michael again.

I was wrong. About practically everything.

And that makes me happy.

The Big Happy

Happiness is bigger than we are. We just have to be open to it. And I don't mean yoga. Yoga was my way back to happiness when I'd lost my capacity for it. But there are other ways as well. For me, happiness is hanging out with my folks, hiking through the woods with our rescue dog Bear, binge-watching HBO with Michael, reading a good book, traveling to Switzerland (the happiest place on Earth, according to some studies) to visit my daughter and granddaughters, sharing a fine meal with my boys, going to book signings with my writer friends, learning to paddleboard, taking in the latest exhibits at MoMA, dancing in the living room all by myself, breathing on my mat.

All roads lead to happiness—you just have to be willing to make the journey.

That's what this book is all about: all the tools and techniques that can help us find meaning and joy in our lives. We can learn to be happy.

Happiness takes practice, just like playing the piano or speaking a foreign language or standing on your head.

We all just want to be happy.
Happier every day.
Starting now.

① Happier at Home

"Happiness is home."
—Dennis Lehane

Home.

Home is where we begin each day and where we return each night. It's where we hang our hats, our hopes, our hearts. It's where we can truly be ourselves, away from the glare of the outside world.

Yet for a surprising number of people, home is not the refuge we want it to be. According to a Penn State study, most people experience less stress—as measured by cortisol levels—at work than at home.

But it doesn't have to be that way. The happiest people come home to welcoming spaces in which they can rest, relax, rejuvenate and recreate—R&R at its best. In this Happier at Home section, we'll explore the ways in which we can create a home environment that nourishes us mentally, physically, emotionally and even spiritually. A place where we can live and love and dream to our heart and soul's content.

Because if you can't be happy in your own home, the rest doesn't matter.

Color Your World

"You have your brush, you have your colors;
you paint the paradise, then in you go."
—Nikos Kazantzakis

THE POWER OF COLOR on our emotions is undeniable—and everyone from advertising executives to restaurateurs use it to evoke feelings that can drive us to buy everything from cars to burgers. Likewise, we can use that power to help us create a happier home. Yellow kitchens are upbeat and cheerful—like mine!—but don't paint your nursery yellow, as babies cry more in yellow rooms. Red is the preferred choice for restaurants because the color is thought to excite the appetite. And blue, considered a soothing and calming color, is often used in bedrooms and bathrooms.

Bestselling novelist Alice Hoffman paints her writing room a color inspired by the novel she's working on at the time. The feeling of the story, so to speak. When I found myself with an empty nest after decades of raising children, I painted my living room a rich cozy cinnamon and immediately felt happier there, cuddled up on my couch on my own.

Think about how certain colors make you feel—and how you can color your world at home to make you feel good.

EXERCISE

Color Your Chakras

Chakras are the energy centers of your body. There are seven main chakras running along your spinal column, from the base of the spine up through the crown of your head. Each is associated with certain colors:

Root Chakra	red, brown	survival/security
Sacral Chakra	orange	sexuality/creativity
Solar Plexus Chakra	yellow	confidence
Heart Chakra	green, pink	love/compassion
Throat Chakra	blue	voice/truth
Third Eye Chakra	violet	intuition
Crown Chakra	white	enlightenment

Choose a room in your house and paint it the color of the quality you'd most like to enhance in your life. For example, if you're writing a novel, paint your writing room blue. Spice up your bedroom—and your sex life—with a coat of orange paint. Encourage happy hanging out with your family and friends by painting your living room green.

A Well-Lit Place

"Light is what gives joy to buildings."
—Jaquelin T. Robertson

SEE THE LIGHT. Light at the end of the tunnel. Light my way. Light my fire. Sweetness and light. Light of day. Ray of light. In a good light. In a bad light. Red light. Green light. Guiding light. Lights on. Lights off. Lights out. Keep the light on for me.

I could go on and on, but you might light into me.

Light has an enormous impact on our emotions, both good and bad. Deprive us of natural light and we get depressed. Drown us in bright light and we get overheated. The right balance of light is critical to our well-being. Many studies of shift workers bear this out, according to *Medical News Today*, revealing that those of us who work outside the 9-to-5 norm interrupt our circadian rhythms, often resulting in lower levels of melatonin and vitamin D, and increased risk of anxiety, depression, bipolar disorder, obesity, insomnia, cardiovascular disease, diabetes, and declining cognitive and memory function. Even those of us working normal daytime hours can suffer from the absence of sunlight and the proliferation of fluorescent light. Not to mention the winter blues (the worst of which is known as seasonal affective disorder), which afflict 1 in every 5 of us.

In other words, in order to be happy and healthy, we need to live in the right kind of light. At least when we're at home. Here are a few ways to light your space properly:

During the day, keep it light and...

    1. Open your curtains.

    2. Use light bulbs that simulate sunlight.

    3. Put in more windows and/or skylights.

    4. Try a (medically approved) light box.

At night, keep it dark and...

    1. Eliminate all sources of outside light.

    2. Switch your screens to night mode (meaning warmer light as opposed to bluer light), or better yet, turn them off altogether.

    3. Lose the night lights, which can contribute to myopia in children and breast cancer in women.

EXERCISE

Let the Light In

Ever since we discovered fire, we've been gathering around the flames for light and warmth and company. Fire allowed us to come out of the trees and sleep safely on the ground, scare away nocturnal predators and cook our own food. This in turn set the stage for pair bonding and even community.

There's a lesson to be learned there from our old pals, the hominids and *Homo erectus*. Light a fire at your house. If you don't have a fireplace, put in a stove. At our little lakeside cottage, we put in a pellet stove, one with a glass front that displayed the flames. The more it snowed, the more we liked it. Best winter ever!

At the very least, get a fire pit for the backyard and have a party. Tell stories and sing songs and roast marshmallows. If you're in an apartment, improvise with candles and warm chocolate cake. Now that's a recipe for a good time.

AROUND THE WORLD IN HAPPY WAYS

And Then There Was Light

"There is no *hygge* without lights."
—Henrik Thierlein

In Denmark, where the devoted pursuit of *hyggeligt*—a kind of highly prized cozy contentment—makes Danes among the happiest people on Earth, lighting is considered critical to creating a happy home. The country boasts some of the most famous lighting designers in the world, and the natives invest heavily in warm lighting, fireplaces and candles to banish the darkness and embrace the light.

Spice the Air

"Smell brings to mind...a family dinner of pot roast and sweet potatoes during a myrtle-mad August in a Midwestern town. Smells detonate softly in our memory like poignant land mines hidden under the weedy mass of years."
—Diane Ackerman

SCENT IS ONE of the most powerful senses we have, particularly when it comes to memory. Think of your favorite scents: the salty exhilaration of the sea, the sweet goodness of your mother's pecan pie, the pheromonal seduction of your lover's cologne. One whiff and you're back at the beach or in your mom's kitchen or in that hotel room in Hawaii.

Your home should smell good. It should smell like petals and pine and peppermint. It should smell like happy memories—even when you've just moved in. That's why realtors bake bread before an open house, better to sell the place. It's an olfactory trick that works like a charm.

Fill your home with scents that remind you of good things and good times. Mix it up: fresh flowers by your bed, a basket of oranges on the kitchen table, pine-scented logs on the fire. Scented candles everywhere.

EXERCISE

The Sweet Smell of Happiness

When you're feeling blue, amp up the perfume. According to *Frontiers in Psychology*, recent studies suggest certain odors can indeed help alleviate certain negative emotional and physical responses. Try citrus for depression; oak leaves (or "green" scents) and roses for stress; lavender for anxiety.

I was going through a particularly stressful time earlier this year: buying a new house, selling my old house, moving, my mother's surgery, a sudden death in the family, my daughter's high-risk pregnancy, a tight deadline on a book, and on and on. During one of the worst days, when I was wondering when and whether this marathon of crises would end, I received an unexpected gift from my pal Michaela: a diffuser with an assortment of essential oils. I filled up the smooth dark cylinder with water, plopped in a few drops of chamomile oil, and turned on the diffuser. The air filled with the peaceful scent and I burst into tears. It was a good cry. And I felt much better. Relieved, relaxed and blessed to have such a generous friend.

Get your own diffuser. Fill the air of your home with the scents that make you smile and cry (in a good way). You'll be happier for it.

Music: The Happiness Muse

"One good thing about music,
when it hits you, you feel no pain."
—Bob Marley

FILL YOUR HOME WITH MUSIC. All kinds of music.
Music acts as a kind of shortcut to our emotions, stimulating our
moods and affecting our brain synapses. Neuroscience studies
at Northwestern University indicate that our bodies are wired to
synchronize with music—think the rhythm of our very
own heartbeats.

It doesn't really matter what kind of music—whatever turns
on the beat in you. Classical music makes your brain happy.
Kirtan music makes your chakras happy. Rock & roll and hip-
hop energize us. Opera, the blues and country music all (to
paraphrase Bob Marley) hit us right in the gut, where—thank
you, John Mellencamp—it "Hurts So Good."

EXERCISE

The Music Rx

Years ago, I found myself in the midst of a heartbreaking situation, with no good way out. I didn't have time for drama, I had a big job and an unfinished house with two teenagers and a toddler. My commuting colleague picked me up one Monday morning after a particularly devastating weekend and I said, "Take me to Kmart. I need wailing women." To his credit, Bob drove me not to work but to the department store. There I loaded up on Patsy Cline ("Crazy") and Janis Joplin ("Me and Bobby McGee") and Mary Chapin Carpenter ("He Thinks He'll Keep Her") and Tina Turner ("What's Love Got To Do With It") and, well, you get the picture. I listened to these songs over and over and over again. These ladies got me through my heartbreak, one wail at a time.

That's the wild cathartic thing about music, according to a study by the University of Missouri: Even sad music makes us feel better—especially when we're feeling sad.

The next time you're feeling down, borrow a tune from my blues songbook and download some wailing women (or lamenting men) of your own. These days, you don't even have to go to Kmart.

Plant a Garden

"And the secret garden bloomed and bloomed
and every morning revealed new miracles."
—Frances Hodgson Burnett

EVERY HOME NEEDS A BIT OF GREEN—be it pots of
geraniums on your kitchen windowsill or raised beds of
vegetables, herbs and flowers in your backyard. When I was
a little girl, I read *The Secret Garden* and desperately wanted
a patch to call my own. But my father was in the Army and
we moved a lot, living in temporary quarters. Not a lifestyle
conducive to gardening. By the time I was 10, we were stationed
in Germany and I was old enough to go to the local market on my
own. The Germans loved plants, especially African violets. I fell
in love with the tiny purple flowering plants. Every Saturday, I
spent all of my allowance on yet another pot of African violets.
They made me happy—they still do. I still keep African violets,
even though I have my own garden now, which blooms and
blooms....

The best part of gardening is playing in the dirt. And the dirtier you get, the better. Dirt, it turns out, is good for you. A University of Bristol study revealed that the friendly bacteria known as *Mycobacterium vaccae,* commonly found in garden soil, alleviates depression by raising serotonin levels in much the same way as Prozac.

There are other benefits as well. A half-hour of gardening can reduce your stress level, improve your mood and boost your self-esteem, according to a study in the *Journal of Health Psychology*. It can also cut your risk of heart disease, stroke and dementia.

So go get dirty.

EXERCISE

Flower Power

Flowers brighten our mood as well as our living space. When we surprise someone with flowers, we're giving the gift of gratitude and happiness, according to a Rutgers University study, which found this boost in positive feelings lasts for days—far longer than gifts of fruit or candles.

Surprise someone in your life with flowers. Buy a dozen roses; give a single bloom to every colleague at your office. And don't forget you: Treat yourself to a flowering plant and place it by your front door to greet you when you come home.

The Joy of Clean

"When all else fails, cleaning house is the perfect antidote to most of life's ills."
—Sue Grafton

I CAN ALWAYS tell the state of my relationship by the state of my kitchen. When I get mad, I clean the kitchen. I bang around the pots and pans, slam cabinet doors, slosh the water around in the sink, drop to my knees and scrub the crap out of the floor. During my first marriage, my kitchen was immaculate. If I hadn't scoured my unhappiness away every day, I may have killed the man. Note: I'm happy—really!—to report that these days my kitchen is clean, but not pathologically spick-and-span.

Cleaning house is not simply therapeutic, it's life-changing. Just ask Marie Kondo, cleaning guru and bestselling author of *The Life-Changing Magic of Tidying Up*. She's made a mint telling people to tidy their way to happiness, and she's not wrong. According to *studyfinds.org*, one study found that people who like keeping a clean house were 25 percent happier than those who did not. One aspect of the research asked participants wearing biometric sensors to enter two rooms, one clean and one dirty. Entering the clean room was associated with improved happiness, lower stress and enhanced critical thinking. But perhaps the most surprising finding of all was that a clean house promotes empathy. This was true even among children, who were 64 percent more likely to be empathetic as adults if they were given cleaning-related chores as a child.

Your mother was right: A clean home is a happy home.

EXERCISE

Play Favorites

The worst thing about cleaning is that it never ends, but the best thing about it is instant gratification. Take your favorite room* in the house and give it a good cleaning from the ground up—floorboards to crown molding. Now make yourself a cup of tea or pour yourself a glass of wine and sit in this room you love and just enjoy it. You earned it.

For extra credit, imagine how lovely it would be to feel this good in every room in your house. You know what to do.

*If your favorite room in the house is the one that's usually the neatest, well, that tells you something.

Lose the Clutter

"At its heart, clutter is a lack of peace."
—Kathi Lipp

WE ARE DROWNING IN CLUTTER. This is not an exaggeration: more than half of all Americans admit to being overwhelmed by the clutter in our lives, according to a study by the National Organization of Professional Organizers, an association of people who make a living helping us throw out our stuff. (My grandmother, who survived the Depression, is rolling her eyes up there in clutter-free heaven.)

The more stuff we have, the more stressed out we are, according to a multi-year study by UCLA's Center on Everyday Lives of Families. This is particularly true of women (who do twice as much housework than men do whether they work outside the home or not, according to the *Journal of Family Theory & Review*—even when their husbands make less money or stay at home).

The solution seems simple enough: Get rid of our stuff.

I read Marie Kondo's book (*The Life-Changing Magic of*

Tidying Up), and I followed her advice to the letter, tossing whatever did not bring me joy. And it worked, except for No. 1, clothes, and No. 2, books. Because nearly all clothes and books bring me joy. I came up with my own solution: Twice a year I invite my friend Susan over and she helps me go through my wardrobe. She's got a keen and cold eye, and with her help I give a lot more to Goodwill than I would on my own. When it comes to books, Susan's not as much help; she's a writer, too, and loves books as much as I do. So we help each other donate books to our local library...some of which we buy back at the library book and bake sale. But at least we try.

EXERCISE

The Junk Drawer

Everyone has a junk drawer. Some of us have more than one. According to Golden Gate University consumer psychologist Kit Yarrow, the junk drawer is one of the most revealing places in the home—a Rorschach test of sorts, capturing what we need, what we think we need and what we can't let go.

Take 10 minutes and clean out your junk drawer. Keep what you need, toss what you only *think* you need and let go of the rest. OK, OK, if you really must keep that old movie stub from that Garbo film you saw with your ex, the one that pulls at your heartstrings every time you open that junk drawer, stash it in a scrapbook. Out of sight, out of mind.

Set the Table and Other Rituals

———

"After a good dinner, one can forgive anybody,
even one's own relatives."
—Oscar Wilde

———

ONE OF THE casualties of modern life is sitting down to dinner. More and more of us eat our meals in front of a screen—the TV, the laptop, the cell phone—forgoing the traditional family meal at the dining table. According to an NYU study, family dinners have declined a whopping 33 percent over the past 20 years.

And yet study after study proves people who sit down to dinner with family and friends are happier, healthier, thinner, stronger—even smarter.

If you have kids, all the more reason to gather around the table for dinner. Children especially benefit from family meals together: Kids who eat with their parents feel more secure, get better grades, have lower rates of drug use and obesity—and they're even less likely to be picky eaters.

Clear off your dining room table, banish the electronics and set the table. Light candles, pour wine, use real plates and real napkins. Fill your plate and pass the salt and talk about your day. (We'll talk more about what to cook for dinner in Part Five: Happier Body.) Whether it's a dinner for one or dinner for five doesn't matter. What matters is that you give your mealtime the respect it—and you—deserve. Bon appétit!

EXERCISE

More Rituals for a Happy Home

One of the most effective ways to simplify your home life is to create rituals around the busiest parts of the day. Mornings can be a nightmare, what with getting yourself and your kids fed and groomed and dressed and off to work and school in a timely, presentable manner. I finally gave up on getting my youngest sleepyhead ready; I simply bathed him the night before and put him in his (permanent press) school clothes instead of pajamas so all he'd have to do is roll out of bed in the morning, brush his teeth and go down to the kitchen table for breakfast.

But you don't have to resort to such tactics.

Start your day by doing this one thing: Make your bed. People who make their beds are not only happier, they get more exercise and more sleep, according to *Psychology Today*.

End your day by doing this one thing: Do the dishes. Washing dishes promotes mindfulness, relaxation and well-being, according to a Florida State University study.

Ritualizing these common chores means no matter what transpires between waking up and going to sleep, you'll begin and end your day with a sense of accomplishment. Plus a neat bed and a clean sink.

AROUND THE WORLD IN HAPPY WAYS

VIVE LA CUISINE FRANÇAISE!

Dis-moi ce que tu manges, je te dirai ce que tu es.
Tell me what you eat and I will tell you what you are.
—French proverb

The French know something about food. Food permeates their culture—the growing of it, the cooking of it, the partaking of it, the sharing of it.

I once spent a flight from California to New York next to a winemaker from Bordeaux. He'd just toured Napa Valley's vineyards and was very enthusiastic about our country. He spoke only French, and so, as I struggled to remember the French I'd learned in college, we conversed about everything he loved about the U.S. He loved our people, he loved our wine, he loved our John Deere tractors. I told him there must be something that he didn't like, say, the food? But he had visited both New Orleans and northern California, so he was fine with our food.

But he did not approve of the way we ate it. "*Dans la voiture,*" he said sadly, shaking his head. "*Dans la voiture.*"

He couldn't believe we ate so many of our meals in the car.

In France, food is an experience to be shared. According to the Crédoc Consumer Studies and Research Institute, the French eat 80 percent of their meals with other people: colleagues,

AROUND THE WORLD IN HAPPY WAYS

family, friends. They're far more likely to go out for dinner than drinks, two-hour lunches are the norm, they rarely snack between meals, they don't bother with children's menus—and they eat more cheese and drink more wine per capita than most other nations.

Which is where the so-called "French paradox" kicks in: Despite the high-fat content of their food, they boast one of the lowest rates of heart disease *and* one of the longest life expectancies in the world. In fact, the culinary culture in France is so *superbe* that in 2010, French cuisine was named to UNESCO's World Heritage List.

I think of that French vintner whenever I go through a drive-through. Americans now eat nearly half of all meals alone, according to a study by the Hartman Group—and Stanford University found that we eat 20 percent of all meals *dans la voiture.*

Which just makes me, uh, *triste.*

And ready to book a flight to Paris.

Create a
Sacred Space

---

*"At first you might find that nothing happens there.
But if you have a sacred space and use it, eventually
something will happen. Your sacred space is where you
can find yourself over and over again."*
—Joseph Campbell

AFTER MANY YEARS in my beloved little lakeside cottage,
where I'd raised kids and written books and stared endlessly
at the moonlight on the water, eventually it came time to move
on. To a new place, one that could accommodate our growing
extended family and our working from home: a historical
Colonial home built in 1760 with a big barn on 19 acres of sugar
maples, complete with its own lake.

We packed up and moved, putting the cottage up for sale. It
sold literally overnight. I loved my big new creative space, a huge
room on the second floor, surrounded by trees and overlooking
the country road and the forest beyond, a delicious bower of a

room with plenty of space in which to write and dream and do yoga. I filled this space with books and candles and pillows and music—all the things that made my cottage so special.

But something was missing. I didn't feel at home, even surrounded by the people and dogs and cats and things that I loved. The day before the closing, I went back to the cottage to clear out the remaining stuff we'd left behind. I walked through the little house, gazing out at the lovely lake view that had been mine for 14 years. But I didn't cry. I sat on the daybed in my small yoga room, painted the same orange as a Buddhist monk's robes and listened to the frogs chanting outside. Still I didn't cry. Then I walked onto the deck out front, into my little picket-fenced garden, with its pergola of lavender wisteria and trellis of red climbing roses and beds of bright-yellow sunflowers and saffron-colored daylilies and snow-white hydrangeas.

And I sat down on one of the red iron benches next to one of my Buddha statues and cried.

This garden, the first patch of green I'd ever really dug that was mine and mine alone, was my sacred space.

I couldn't take the flowers and shrubs and vines, but I could take my Buddhas and my benches. I lugged all my garden ornaments into my Jeep and brought them to the old Colonial. In the 258 years since this place was built, it's never seen a Buddha garden. But it's got one now. And that's just the beginning.

Figure out what your sacred space looks like. Create it. If it makes you cry with happiness, you know you've got it right.

EXERCISE

Claim a Corner

You don't need 19 acres to create your sacred space. All you need is a little corner in your house or garden where you can connect to your higher self, honor your traditions, whatever they may be, and dream your wildest dreams. The key is to create a space that evokes all your senses.

- Music
- Pillows
- Books
- Posters
- Candles
- Icons
- Photos

Remember, this is your space; fill it with whatever speaks to you. Try to spend some time there every day, even if it's only 15 minutes in the morning and 15 minutes before bed. That's enough time to light a candle, say a prayer, chant a mantra, do a down dog, read a poem, write in your journal, sit in seated pose.

Take a deep breath. You're home.

Have a Party

"I believe when life gives you lemons, you should make lemonade...then find someone whose life is giving them vodka, and have a party."
—Ron White

HANGING OUT WITH FRIENDS is what happy people do. That's because people with the most social connections are the happiest people, as reported in the famous Framingham Heart Study.

Spending time with your friends and family can make you happy, too, especially if you hang with happy people, according to *Personality and Social Psychology Bulletin*.

Happiness is contagious. So, invite your friends over. You don't have to hire a band or host a sit-down dinner for 20 people. Just ask a couple of friends to drop by for movie night and pizza. Barbecue and beer. *Trivial Pursuit* and G&Ts.

For extra credit, make it a regular date. Volunteer to host book club meetings or *D&D* games or poker night once a month—or more.

EXERCISE

Start an Entertainment Tradition

Whatever your favorite holiday, celebrate it by sharing it with the people you love. At your house. Make it a tradition, an event everyone in your circle of family and friends looks forward to every year. Here's a list of possibilities. Choose one that's right for you:

- New Year's Day brunch
- Halloween costume contest
- Oscar night party
- Oktoberfest beer bash
- Fourth of July barbecue
- Run for the Roses tea

②

Happier at Work

"Your work is going to fill a large part of your life, and the only way to be truly satisfied is to do what you believe is great work. And the only way to do great work is to love what you do. If you haven't found it yet, keep looking. Don't settle."
—Steve Jobs

For most of us, work consumes the better part of every day. Americans work longer hours than most anybody—137 hours more a year than the Japanese, 260 more hours a year than the Brits and more than 499 hours a year than the French, according to the International Labour Organization.

If you're thinking it's time to move to France, well, maybe. (Croissants, Bordeaux, a 35-hour work week and five weeks minimum annual vacation—what's not to like? Talk about *joie de vivre*.)

Flying off to Paris may not be possible, or even desirable. But if we are going to work so much—more than 40 hours a week and five or more hours a weekend for many of us, according to the Bureau of Labor Statistics—we should at least try to enjoy it. Yet more than half of all Americans are not happy with their jobs, according to a Conference Board study.

As the sort of person who loves her work, the times when I've been unhappy at a job have been few—but looking back, I can see that I stayed in those jobs way too long. When I got laid off and found myself middle-aged and unemployable, I never thought I'd be happy again.

Wrong.

I'm busier—and happier—than ever. I'm self-employed now, and like most self-employed people, I work longer hours than ever before, but that doesn't bother me. As Confucius pointed out centuries ago, choose a job you love, and you will never have to work a day in your life.

How do you find a job that makes you happy? In this next section, we'll explore all of the factors that play into satisfaction on the job.

So you can follow your bliss, one shift at a time.

Be a Leader

"Leadership is not about a title or a designation.
It's about impact, influence and inspiration."
—Robin S. Sharma

YOU DON'T HAVE to be a manager or a supervisor to be a leader. You don't even have to be part of a team. You can work at home on your own and still be a leader by impacting, influencing and inspiring your colleagues, clients and customers, and reaping the benefits of that impact, influence and inspiration.

This can be as simple as when you:

- Compliment a coworker on a job well done
- Brainstorm solutions with a client
- Help a colleague prepare a presentation
- Share your best practices with a new hire
- Advise a customer on new business strategies
- Give a speech at an industry conference
- Volunteer to head up a new project
- Organize a corporate fundraiser
- Help run a work retreat

Such leadership in action is as good for you as it is for the people you're helping. In fact, research shows that while it's long been accepted that mentees benefit from these associations with encouraging and supportive colleagues, mentors too enjoy higher levels of job performance, job satisfaction and career success than their non-mentoring peers, according to the *Journal of Vocational Behavior.*

EXERCISE

Choose a Protégé

Taking a fellow worker under your wing is a great way to build your leadership skills and get happy on the job at the same time. You could start small, by volunteering to show the new intern around the office or treating your favorite junior colleague to lunch and chat about her career goals. Or you can go big, asking the most overlooked and underappreciated work horse—every office has one—to work on a project with you, one that will bring him or her a little much-needed glory. If you don't work in an office, or telecommute or work for yourself, offer to mentor a local high school student interested in your line of work or sign up as an online mentor for your industry association.

As the Buddhist saying goes, "When the student is ready, the teacher appears." I've been blessed with so many fabulous mentors over the course of my life that it would take another book to acknowledge and thank them all properly. I dedicated this book to two of them, my yoga teacher Emma Spencer Boyle and my yoga teacher trainer Michelle Fleming. I try to honor all of my teachers by paying it forward.

We never really know how what we do affects people; we can only hope that the results of our actions are kind and good and helpful. Happy, even.

Foster Creativity

"You can't use up creativity.
The more you use, the more you have."
—Maya Angelou

THE MORE CREATIVE YOU ARE, the happier you are. That's because creativity is basically play. Playing at work pays off, and not just in job satisfaction. The World Economic Forum reports that creativity is one of the top skills employers are looking for - right after problem-solving and critical thinking, both of which require creativity. In fact, the majority of CEOs say creativity is the skill they value most in employees, according to *U.S. News & World Report.*

We spend a lot of time at work and yet 75 percent of us believe we are not living up to our creative potential, according to a global-benchmark study by Adobe. More and more companies are recognizing this and doing all they can to encourage workers to think outside the box. At Google, engineers spend 20 percent of their work week pursuing projects of their own choosing, projects that reflect their own personal and professional passions (think Gmail, one of the many results of this policy).

Whether you work for one of these forward-thinking companies or not, you can weave more creativity-enhancing moments into your workday, like these below, all of which are thought to boost creativity:

1. Focus on breathing.
2. Listen to classical music.
3. Make a list of the things you are passionate about.
4. Read.
5. Keep an idea notebook.

EXERCISE

Get Out of the Office

Sometimes the best way to jump-start the creative process is to get out of Dodge. If you're a manager or supervisor or team leader, organize a meeting off-site. When I was in acquisitions, responsible for leading the content team that came up with new ideas for books and more, I would host brainstorming sessions at my little lakeside cabin, and the entire editorial department would come and hang out by the lake, throwing out ideas and dreaming up solutions to problems we were experiencing back at the office. These biannual meetings always produced great ideas that, in time, became books, calendars, series, web content and more.

You don't have to be in management to enhance your own creativity or that of your peers. You may not be able to dedicate 20 percent of your work week to brainstorming, but at the very least, you've got lunch. Put the phone down and spend your PB&J time in a nearby park, daydreaming ideas on your own. Or better yet, invite a colleague along.

Play to Your Strengths

"Draw the art you want to see, start the business you want to run, play the music you want to hear, write the books you want to read, build the products you want to use—do the work you want to see done."
—Austin Kleon

THOSE OF US who are the happiest and most successful at work play to our strengths. We are not only more productive, we are more energetic and less stressed out. We sleep better, learn more, suffer less anger and physical pain. We even laugh and smile more.

Seriously.

As it turns out, the key to success and job satisfaction is not focusing on our weaknesses, but rather playing to our strengths. This is covered in study after study, most notably a recent Gallup report involving more than a million workers.

You know what your strengths are: they're those skills and qualities that reflect what you like to do most, what you tend to do well and what you'd do even if they didn't pay you to do it. You know when you're playing to your strengths because you feel enlivened and engaged. You feel like your best self.

Be your best self. Play to your strengths. Be happier on the job.

EXERCISE

List Your Strengths

Take 10 minutes and make a list of your strengths. Don't stop until you've come up with at least a dozen, preferably two dozen. Don't focus just on skills, like "I'm a good writer" or "I'm good at building financial models." List your character strengths (wisdom, kindness, perseverance, etc.) and your personality strengths (charm, humor, confidence, etc.) as well.

If you have trouble coming up with things, search for online surveys and take one. Two you might try are the (free) VIA Inventory of Strengths and the (fee-based) Gallup CliftonStrengths assessment.

Or simply sit down with your best friend or favorite colleague. Make a list of your BFF's or peer's strengths while she does the same for you. Then, exchange lists and discuss.

The results may surprise you. I am always somewhat astonished when people tell me they envy my confidence. I don't think of myself as a particularly confident person, and decades later I still have to steel myself whenever I walk into a room of strangers. Flash back to always being the new kid at school. I learned back then to fake it—or eat lunch alone for the rest of my life. Apparently, that worked.

Engage Your Coworkers

"Time for reflection with colleagues is, for me,
a lifesaver; it is not just a nice thing to do if you
have the time. It is the only way you can survive."
—Margaret J. Wheatley

WORK IS MORE FUN when you work with people you like.
This may sound obvious, but if you need proof, a study in
the *Journal of Business and Psychology* revealed that we're
happier and more productive at work when we have friends at
work. Duh.

But having friends at work is not the given it used to be.
In 1985, half of Americans had at least one close friend at work.
Now, according to a study by the Ross School of Business, we
are far less likely to make such friends. Only 30 percent of us
have one close friend at work. Not to mention many of us work
alone anyway.

This lack of engagement worries the Joint Economic Committee of the U.S. Congress, which issued a report called *What We Do Together* bemoaning this trend. It should worry us too.

EXERCISE

Teatime for Overachievers

I started off as a reporter, working in a big noisy newsroom packed with desks and people yelling into their landlines. I liked the hubbub and the camaraderie and the general congenial chaos of it all.

Fast forward several years to my new job as an acquisitions editor for a publisher specializing in books about design and architecture (I did the decorating books). It was the quietest office I'd ever encountered. So quiet that I was considered a threat to the peace and tranquility of this hushed environment because I talked and—God forbid—laughed too loud. They were nice people, truly, but they were *very quiet people*.

They put me in my own office, a small windowless room with all of the charm of a prison cell and a door they expected me to keep shut, the better to confine my boisterousness. I couldn't work in there as it was, so I brought in my own art and lamps and easy chairs. I also brought in my own electric tea kettle and a cookie jar, and every afternoon at 3 p.m. I made a pot of Earl Grey tea and took the lid off the jar. Tea time for *moi*.

Eventually, word got around. People started dropping by every afternoon for a cuppa and a Lorna Doone cookie. I started opening my door around 3 in the afternoon every day, ultimately befriending most of my colleagues. No one complained. As it turned out, even *very quiet people* like teatime.

Try teatime at your workplace. If you work alone, invite a pal to meet you at Starbucks. Or go on your own and make friends with your fellow working coffee drinkers.

Note: The more you don't want to do this, the more you probably should.

Unplug

"In barely one generation, we've moved from exulting in time-saving devices that have so expanded our lives, to trying to get away from them—often in order to make more time. The more ways we have to connect, the more many of us seem desperate to unplug."
—Pico Iyer

THE GOOD NEWS IS technology makes work portable; the bad news is you can't get away from it, no matter where you go (remote mountain ranges aside). This tech takeover contributes to the growing rate of burnout—a whopping 81 percent of us and counting suffer its symptoms, according to Monster Worldwide.

But it doesn't have to be that way, and it shouldn't be.

If you want to get any substantive work done—writing, creating, problem-solving—you need to spend some time each day at work unplugged. Here are some tips to help you do that:

Put away your phone. It's the ultimate distraction and it never stops.

Take off those ear buds. You can't pay attention to two different things at once without disrespecting one of them.

Restrict email, texts and messages. Limit your checking of these interruptions—and that's what they are—to three times a day. If you're worried about your kids or your boss or your mom, give them special rings/tones/whatever so on the off chance that there really is an emergency, you're available.

Turn off that screen. Studies from the University of Toronto and the National Sleep Foundation indicate that too much exposure to blue screens can lead to blindness and insomnia. Limit your screen time and use your night mode (to warmer light) all the time.

Do one thing at a time. Multitasking is a misnomer; our brains can't do it. What we're really doing is just forcing ourselves to switch gears too rapidly, contributing to higher stress levels.

EXERCISE

Because It's the Weekend, People

"What is a weekend?"
—Lady Violet, Dowager Countess of Grantham, *Downton Abbey*

Fewer and fewer of us know what a weekend is these days—and not because we're part of Lady Violet's leisure class. It's because we can't stop working, even when we want to, because the never-ending barrage of texts, emails, voicemails and messages won't let us.

Most of us work weekends these days, according to *Forbes*. And I am no exception. But I do make Sunday my version of a day of rest, which means I give myself permission to do only what I feel like doing on this one day a week. Sometimes all I feel like doing is binge-watching Netflix. Or taking my dog on a long walk through the woods. Or sleeping. But if I feel like reading manuscripts or answering emails or writing another chapter, I do. But if not, no worries and no guilt. If anyone I did not give birth to (or gave birth to me) texts, I give myself permission to ignore it until Monday morning.

Because it's the weekend, people.

Try it. You'll like it.

Focus

———

"It's hard to edit. It's hard to stay focused.
And yet, we know we'll only do our best work if we
stay focused. And so, you know, the hardest decisions
we made are all the things not to work on, frankly."
—Tim Cook

———

AS HUMAN BEINGS, we are easily driven to distraction.
The average human attention span tops out at eight seconds—
down from 12 seconds in 2000 and dropping as we speak,
thanks to everything digital as well as our own in-search-of-
novelty brains. Even goldfish can focus longer than we can (an
astounding nine seconds!) according to a Microsoft study.

I know, I know, you're wondering what goldfish have to
focus on in that little bowl, and why am I not defending you and
your fellow humans, because, come on, our little bowl is way
bigger and more distracting than theirs.

But we digress.

Which is the whole point. Unfortunately, it may take us an

average of 25 minutes to regain our focus once lost, reports a study from the University of California, Irvine.

Let's get back on track: People who can focus are happier at work because they get more done. People who get more done enjoy a greater sense of accomplishment and, ultimately, success. In fact, the ability to focus is one of the character traits associated with higher achievers, according to *Psychology Today*.

These can help you enhance your powers of concentration:

1. Listen to the sounds of silence. Wear headphones—without music—or use a white noise system to block out unwanted noise.
2. Before you sit down to work, take a walk or do some gentle exercise.
3. Shut the door. If you can't get any privacy at the office, work at a nearby coffee shop or library.
4. Put your autoresponders on and stay off email and social media for a designated period.
5. Make a to-do list before you begin so you're not thinking about everything else you need to do. List it and forget it...for now.

EXERCISE

The Hourglass

Writing anything requires complete focus. As a writer, I'm often faced with a blank page and a deadline. If I can't concentrate, I can't write. When I find myself doing anything but writing—raiding the fridge, texting my pals, watching cat videos—I turn over the hourglass on my desk and write until the sand runs out. By the time it does, I'm off and running myself.

Try it. You don't need an hourglass (but they are cool). You can just set an egg timer or the alarm on your phone for 30 minutes (remembering that it can take 25 minutes to get back down to business). Promise yourself that you'll focus on the task in front of you for just half an hour.

Half an hour. And you'll be off and running too.

⊣ HAPPY PILLS ⊢

Concentrate on Caffeine

"Coffee: creative lighter fluid."
—Floyd Maxwell

There's a reason you kick-start your morning with a cup of espresso and shake off your mid-afternoon slump with a double iced latte: caffeine.

Caffeine triggers the fight or flight response, and if you're not fighting or fleeing but rather sitting at your computer trying to work, all that adrenaline and norepinephrine primes your body for action, boosting blood flow, firing off neurotransmitters and oxygenating your blood—setting the stage for enhanced focus and concentration.

So go ahead, have another cup of coffee—and if you're really dragging, add a bit of sugar and enjoy a higher blood glucose level as well. Double whammy!

Goal Setting for Optimists

"A goal properly set is half reached."
—Zig Ziglar

IF YOU THINK THAT setting goals is a recipe for disappointment and disaster, think again. Whenever you set a goal and meet it, you also set off your dopamine system of achievement and reward. Dopamine is the neurotransmitter that makes us feel good when we get what we want, in this case, a goal achieved. This is why we love checking items off our to-do lists—every time we do, our brains are rewarded with a flood of dopamine.

That's right, the same dopamine associated with addiction can help you make your dreams both large and small come true. The trick is to set the right goals. That is, the goals that will trigger a release of dopamine.

There are two kinds of goals: zero sum goals and non-zero

sum goals. Zero sum goals are all about you: fame, fortune, etc. ("I will do a TED talk." or "I will write a bestseller.") Non-zero sum goals are not about making you rich or famous, but rather about making you feel more independent, more competent and more connected to other people. ("I will volunteer at a Boys & Girls Club once a week." or "I will teach a free class at the library that helps people manage their finances.")

Take a look at your goals and figure out which are non-zero sum and which are zero sum goals. Find a way to rework those zero sum goals into non-zero sum goals.

Not surprisingly, studies show people who focus on non-zero sum goals tend to be more content.

Plus, think of all the dopamine.

EXERCISE

Go Forth and Be Your Best Possible Self

The best thing about goals is they don't have to be grand. Your goals should be a mix of modest and ambitious objectives. The bigger the goal, the smaller the steps you'll need to get there.

Take half an hour and write about your future self, a future in which you have realized all your goals, large and small. What does your life look like? Write it all down.

Just doing this Best Possible Self exercise can improve your mood, boost your short term happiness and make you more optimistic.

Laugh

"We don't laugh because we are happy,
we are happy because we laugh."
—William James

LAUGH, AND THE WORLD LAUGHS WITH YOU—thanks to the release of endorphins that floods your brain when you laugh, and a similar release in the brains of those laughing with you. Laughter is contagious.

It's also good for your career. If you've got a sense of humor, you're more likely to be seen as doing a good job and worthy of advancement by your colleagues, according to a study by Robert Half International. In fact, a Bell Leadership Institute study revealed that humor coupled with a strong work ethic constitute the two most important traits in leaders.

Humor is the secret weapon of the workplace. You can use it to befriend colleagues, defuse tension, bond teams, improve communication, facilitate negotiations, boost creativity, build trust, brainstorm solutions to problems and even sell more of whatever it is your business sells.

So go ahead and laugh—all the way to the bank.

EXERCISE

A Laugh a Minute

It's often said that comedy is tragedy plus time. Make a list of the funniest things that have ever happened to you at work. How many of these things did you actually think were funny at the time they happened? How has time changed your perspective?

Now make a second list where you itemize the times you or a colleague failed to see the humor in the situation. Times when, had you or she laughed, everything could have been different. What lessons have you learned about humor, and how will you benefit from those lessons going forward?

Be Open

"A mind is like a parachute.
It doesn't work if it is not open."
—Frank Zappa

OPEN-MINDEDNESS IS ONE OF THE most sought-after traits in new hires, according to the University of California, Davis Internship and Career Center. No surprise there, as open-minded people tend to be more flexible, adaptable, cooperative, curious and creative. Not to mention no one likes a know-it-all—and open-minded people know they don't know it all.

Open-minded people literally *see* the world differently. According to a study in the *Journal of Research in Personality*, open-minded people are able to integrate disparate images in a way that close-minded people cannot; that is, their visual perception of reality is not the same as their close-minded peers. They are able to see two different images at the same time, where their more narrow-minded peers can only process one image at a time. This ability is linked to creativity, where making connections between very different things is key to the creative process.

What do you see when you look at your world: problems or possibilities?

The answer to this question affects your job satisfaction and your level of success. Think about how being more open-minded at work might open doors for you. Observe your most open-minded colleagues—and take notes. Challenge your own assumptions, monitor your reactions, look for opportunity where you once saw difficulty.

Open your mind, and watch your world change right before your eyes.

EXERCISE

Pull a George Costanza

Part of being open-minded—some would argue the most important part—is being open to new experiences. I think of George Costanza from *Seinfeld*. If there was ever a character stuck in his ways, it's George. In my favorite *Seinfeld* episode of all time, "The Opposite," Jerry advises George to do the opposite of what he would normally do, since what he would normally do never works. George does, and by the end of the episode, well, I won't ruin it for you. Suffice it to say that being open-minded enough to embrace new ways of doing things can really pay off.

Pull a Costanza. For the next 24 hours, do the opposite of what you would normally do. Change your reactions to people, places, things. Try something new. Choose the road less traveled.

And see where it takes you.

Speak Up

———

"I'm trying to elevate small talk to medium talk."
—Larry David

———

HAPPY PEOPLE don't necessarily talk more than other (unhappier) people, but what they talk about is different. In an intriguing University of Arizona study, researchers found that happy people have more substantive conversations than unhappy people.

While there's nothing wrong with talking about sports or the weather or the route you drove to get where you were going (the three staples of small talk where I live in New England), those conversations are not as rewarding as those in which both people involved in the dialogue learn something new about one another and/or deepen their understanding of one another.

These meaningful interactions are the hallmark of happy people, at work, at home and in the world at large.

Ask yourself how you can communicate more meaningfully at work. Think about the most meaningful conversations you've had with your boss, your team, your colleagues. Broaden your approach to substantive dialogue and aim for at least two such conversations a day. We're not talking about baring your soul here, but simply taking even the most superficial interactions with people to a deeper level.

Hint: This works best in person. If you're telecommuting, opt for video calls rather than phone calls or emails, as they're the next best thing to in-person interactions.

EXERCISE

Go Deep with Small Talk

Think of small talk as a gateway drug to meaningful conversation. With practice, you can take any dialogue to a deeper level. Here are some tips and tricks:

1. Put away your phones.
2. Listen more than you talk.
3. Pose open-ended questions, those that often begin with why or how.
4. Steer clear of your favorite subjects (which may find you blathering on and on).
5. When in doubt, ask for advice.

Now, invite your most introverted colleague at work to lunch. Use the techniques you've learned to get to know this person a little better.

Note: If you're the most introverted at work, seek out a more extroverted colleague you admire and do the same.

Find Your Flow

"The happiest people spend much time in a state of flow—the state in which people are so involved in an activity that nothing else seems to matter; the experience itself is so enjoyable that people will do it even at great cost, for the sheer sake of doing it."
—Mihaly Csikszentmihalyi

YOU KNOW THE FEELING. You start doing something—writing, running, coding—and the next thing you know it's hours and miles and lines later. You've lost track of your time and your surroundings and everything else—except what you're doing. You're in the moment. You're in the effort. You're in the zone.

Study after study shows being happy at work means spending more time in the zone. If you're not happy, then try this seven-step process:

1. Choose a task you're good at and enjoy but that's challenging enough to require your full effort.
2. Visualize yourself acing that task.

3. Block out at least an hour during your most productive time of the day.
4. Close your door and turn off your phone.
5. Do that task.
6. Repeat every day and record your daily progress.
7. Have fun!

EXERCISE

Your Moment of Zone

You don't have to be an athlete to get in the zone. You just have to prepare the way an athlete prepares for the big game. Show up. Practice. Commit. Flow is a byproduct of hard work and emotion. If you don't love what you're doing, you'll never get in the zone. This means spending more time at work doing the tasks you like most and using the skills you most value. According to the "father of flow" Mihaly Csikszentmihalyi, people who experience flow on a regular basis are the people who modify their jobs to enhance flow and have more fun.

You can do the same, starting today. Make time for a pet project. Schedule a call with your favorite client. Brainstorm new ideas with a creative colleague.

Whatever it takes to go with the flow.

⊢ AROUND THE WORLD IN HAPPY WAYS ⊢

ARBEJDSGLÆDE: HAPPINESS AT WORK

Arbejdsglæde is a Scandinavian word that means "happiness at work"—from *arbejde* meaning "work" and *glæde* meaning "happiness." It's the only word of its kind, and exists only in Danish, Swedish, Norwegian, Finnish and Icelandic. The fact that only the Scandinavians name this feeling may have something to do with these nations typically topping the list of the world's happiest workers, as ranked by Universum's Happiness Index:

1. Denmark
2. Norway
3. Costa Rica
4. Sweden
5. Austria
6. Netherlands
7. Finland
8. Belgium
9. Hungary
10. Czech Republic

The top 10—the U.S. came in 36th—were determined by surveying more than 200,000 workers around the world using a scoring system ranking their job satisfaction, whether they would recommend their company to others and whether they were likely to leave the company in the near future.

———

"You are never too old to set another
goal or to dream a new dream."
—C.S. Lewis

———

③

Happier Alone

——

"I find it wholesome to be alone the greater part of the time. To be in company, even with the best, is soon wearisome and dissipating. I love to be alone. I never found the companion that was so companionable as solitude."
—Henry David Thoreau

——

Solitude is the antidote to our 24/7, 21st century lives. It's a gift, a grace, a practice. Being alone gives us the time and space we need to breathe, to think, to dream and to push ourselves to greater physical, emotional, even spiritual heights...or to do absolutely nothing at all. Ask any writer or runner or artist or monk.

But there's alone, and then there's lonely. Too many of us are lonely; nearly half of all Americans feel lonely or left out some if not all of the time, with young people particularly vulnerable to loneliness, according to a recent study by Cigna.

Happy people know the difference between alone and lonely, acknowledging the comforts of community but actively cultivating the joys of solitude as well. This means learning to enjoy your own company, which is critical to maintaining a strong sense of self and well-being, according to the *Journal for the Theory of Social Behaviour*. The conventional wisdom that you need to be happy on your own before you can be happy with someone else is true.

In this section, we'll explore how solitude can enhance your life, and the many ways in which you can enjoy the benefits of solitude.

Because when it comes to being truly happy, the buck stops with you.

Articulate
Your Mission

———

"Everyone has his own specific vocation or mission in life; everyone must carry out a concrete assignment that demands fulfillment. Therein he cannot be replaced, nor can his life be repeated, thus, everyone's task is unique as is his specific opportunity to implement it."
—Viktor E. Frankl

———

CALL IT A MISSION STATEMENT, a vision statement or just a plain old slogan. Every company worth its salt has one, usually defined in only a few words. Apple: Think different. TED: Ideas worth spreading. Disneyland: The happiest place on Earth.

You are a company of one: You, Inc. You need a mission statement, too, one that defines who you really are at your core. What drives you, what matters to you, who you want to be when you grow up. In other words, your life purpose.

People with a strong *raison d'être* enjoy what psychologists call eudaimonic well-being. Rooted in meaning and self-realization, this is a deeper and longer-lasting sort of contentment than that based on pleasure and pain avoidance, according to research conducted at the University of Rochester.

That's not all. Those of us with a sense of purpose are also healthier physically and emotionally; we sleep better, have fewer strokes and heart attacks, and are less likely to suffer from depression, dementia and disability. We live longer and—wait for it—we even make more money, according to a study in the *Journal of Research in Personality*.

Only a fraction of us strongly endorse the idea of meaning, much less pursue it. Maybe that's because figuring out your life purpose is an inside job. Only you can do it. Create a mission statement for yourself. Know your purpose, commit to it and act on it—and you'll be happier, healthier, wealthier and maybe even wiser.

EXERCISE

Make a Vision Board

If you're not sure what your mission is, create a vision board. You can use poster paper and pictures from magazines, or you can create a collage on your computer or Pinterest. Gather images and text that appeal to the you whom you aspire to be.

When I found myself in an empty nest after my kids had grown and gone, I needed a new *raison d'être*. I made a vision board, and when it was finished I was surprised to find three themes emerge: books, yoga and dogs, which basically describes my life today as I live it, on and off the mat. My mission statement, as it were.

Do a Home Practice

"You are the sky, everything else is just the weather."
—Pema Chodron

DOING A HOME PRACTICE is one of the best ways to embrace your solitude. When you're alone, you have the means and the opportunity to practice your way, at your own time and your own pace, according to your own preferences.

Your home practice doesn't have to be yoga; you can meditate or do tai chi or read tarot cards, or simply slip outside and gaze at the stars. What matters is whatever your home practice is, it should soothe your spirit and speak to your soul. For me, it's all about yoga. I go to classes led by my favorite teachers whenever I can, but like most yoga practitioners in the U.S., I do more yoga at home than anywhere else.

Good for *moi*, because as it turns out, those of us who practice our yoga at home enjoy greater well-being and mindfulness. We sleep better, suffer less fatigue, eat more fruits and vegetables, and are more likely to be vegetarians, according to a study published in *Evidence-based Complementary and Alternative Medicine*. How often we practice at home is a far better indicator of overall positive health than how many classes we go to or how long we've been practicing.

Choose a home practice. Set aside a corner to sit zazen, make room for a mat, lay your tarot cards out on a special table. Practice every day. Tune out the world and tune into your higher self.

Because there really is no place like home.

EXERCISE

Have Mat, Will Travel

Doing a home practice doesn't mean you can only do it at home. A practice is portable; you can take it with you wherever you go. I travel a great deal. Given the rigors of the road—jet lag, haphazard meals, lumpy hotel beds, long hours, too much sitting and standing and schmoozing and networking—I need yoga more than ever. A friend gave me a mat carrier that doubles as an overnight bag, and now I take my mat with me on my travels. Wherever I am, I just roll it out and voila!—the neck strain and back pain and monkey mind are gone.

The next time you're on the road, take your practice with you. This way, you can come home to your higher self, no matter where you lay your head at night.

Find Your Happy Place

"To go out with the setting sun on an empty beach
is to truly embrace your solitude."
—Jeanne Moreau

EVERYONE HAS A HAPPY PLACE. For some, it's the call of
the wild; for others, it's the call of big-city culture. Hint:
You know it's your happy place if you can go there by yourself
and love every minute of it. It's where you can be alone and not
feel lonely. Wherever your happy place is, you need to go there
more often.

When I was a young woman and going through a very painful
divorce, I was living in California about a two-hour drive from
the beach. Every Saturday when my soon-to-be ex-husband
came to get the kids for his weekend visitation, I kissed them
goodbye and then got in my car and drove to Capitola, just south
of Santa Cruz.

This alarmed my father, who thought I was going wild at the beach. One weekend, he came along and sat with me on the hot sand, soaking up the sun, breathing in the sea air and thinking about absolutely nothing.

"Is this all you do here?"

"Yep."

He smiled, obviously relieved. "I get it. You go to the beach the way I go to the woods."

He was right. The beach is my happy place. At least one of them—I also love the woods and bookstores and museums and concerts and coffee shops.

No matter where your happy place is, it's good for you to go there. (We'll talk more about this in the section on Happier Brain on page 164.) Suffice it to say that study after study shows happy places are good for your body, mind and spirit.

Find your happy place. Go there often.

Note: If you have trouble locating a happy place, think back to your childhood. The summers on the beach, the camping trips with your family, the road trips to see that giant ball of string. Wherever you enjoyed going as a child, seek out that place. Tap into that same source. Let the child in you remember, and let the adult in you play.

EXERCISE

Your Happiest Place on Earth

For years, I carried around my passport in my purse just in case I had a really bad day and needed to board the next flight to Paris. Where is your ultimate happy place? Where would you go if you had a really bad day and could hop on the next plane? Make a list of all the places you've ever dreamed about going—places you're happy to go on your own. Go there.

Eventually I went to the City of Light. For me, Paris remains the perfect city. When I'm strolling her streets, I feel like Baudelaire's *flâneur*—awake, alive and part of something bigger than myself.

Take Up a Solo Sport

"There is nothing so good for the inside of a man
as the outside of a horse."
—John Lubbock

AFTER MY SECOND DIVORCE, I found myself alone a lot
while my son was visiting his father. The hurt and loneliness
I felt during these times was overwhelming, so I did the only
sensible thing I could think of: I took up horseback riding.

I'd learned to ride as a child, and I'd always wanted my
own horse. That never happened because we moved so much
during my childhood. But now I was stuck in California for the
foreseeable future and I figured I may as well indulge my inner
child, even if I was middle-aged. I hadn't been on a horse in
decades, but that didn't stop me. I bought myself some breeches
and a velvet helmet, joined a local stable, saddled up and rode off

my troubles on a beautiful black quarter horse with a white blaze named, well, Blaze.

If you're not the team sports type or if you prefer to work out alone or if you just aren't up to being with people, take up a solo sport. (The benefits are too many to count, but we'll try in the upcoming Happier Body, Happier Brain and Happier Heart sections, on pages 132, 164, and 198, respectively.) Here's a list of options to get you started:

• Surfing	• Ice-skating	• Running
• Sailing	• Biking	• Snowshoeing
• Swimming	• Hiking	• Rock climbing
• Skiing	• Kayaking	• Weight training
• Paddleboarding	• Archery	• Fishing
• Horseback riding	• Rollerblading	• Walking
• Snowboarding	• Trampolining	• Skateboarding

EXERCISE

Going Solo in a Group

Just because you've taken up an individual sport doesn't mean you have to do it alone. You may find that you are more motivated when you work out with other people, and may exercise longer and with more intensity, according to studies in the *Journal of Sport and Exercise Psychology* and by the Society of Behavioral Medicine, among others. The good news is, classes abound at your local gym or YMCA. Pick a style and go:

- Spinning
- Kickboxing
- CrossFit
- Zumba

- Tap dancing
- Pilates
- Barre
- Yoga

- Martial arts
- Water aerobics

If you don't want to venture out of the house, try one of the many streaming workouts available online. Just do it!

Read a Book

"We read to know we're not alone."
—William Nicholson

BOOKS HAVE ALWAYS BEEN MY FRIENDS.
Whenever I was lonely—and as an only child and the perennial new kid at school, that was fairly often—I turned to books for companionship. As an adult, I read and write for a living. Books are literally the tools of my trade. And yet, whenever I have a spare minute, I read a new book. It's fun—and it's really good for me. Reading boosts brain power, makes us more empathetic and may even help fight Alzheimer's. In fact, people who read are two-and-a-half times less likely to develop Alzheimer's, according to a *Proceedings of the National Academy of Sciences* study. Reading is also a serious stress-buster, reducing stress levels by as much as 68 percent, says a University of Sussex study.

Can't sleep? Read a printed book and you'll doze off, according to Mayo Clinic. Read literary fiction and you'll even become more empathic, researchers at University of Buffalo found.

I can attest to the instructive, empathetic power of books. I'm not much of a club person, but when my favorite writer, Alice Hoffman, agreed to host a book club meeting, I signed up immediately. The book was *Wuthering Heights.* I never liked that novel much, but I read the book (again) and this time the story really resonated with me. I saw many parallels between me and my ex and Cathy and Heathcliff. That understanding may have set the stage for our reconciliation several years later. One never knows.

Spend time with your favorite characters, escaping to new places here and beyond. You'll learn more about the world and yourself.

EXERCISE

Once More, with Feeling

As we've seen, reading a print book before bed can help you go to sleep. Keep a stack of books by your bed—preferably old favorites that you can turn to again and again. Include some of your favorite books from childhood. Experience them once more, tapping into the emotions you felt when you first read it so long ago.

And then dream happy dreams.

Adopt a Pet

"Until one has loved an animal,
a part of one's soul remains unawakened."
—Anatole France

IF YOU'VE EVER HAD a cat curl up in your lap or a dog waiting
for you, tail wagging, when you walk in the door, you know
that when you share your life with a pet, you're never really
alone. Science backs that up: Having a pet assuages loneliness,
particularly for older people and single women, as reported in
studies by UCLA and UC Davis, respectively.

Get a dog and you'll suffer less depression, lower blood
pressure and lower cholesterol, according to the American Heart
Association.

Get a cat and you'll enjoy a 40 percent lower risk of
heart attack and stroke, along with lower levels of stress and
loneliness, a University of Minnesota study found. According
to one study in *Anthrozoös*, having a cat can provide the same
positive effect as having a romantic partner. So there.

I got my first cat when I was 5 years old, a lovely Siamese

named Johnnie Bonnie Munier (I was 5). My poodle Rogue was my birthday surprise when I turned 10. I've adopted many cats and dogs ever since. As I write this (and, I suspect, as you read it) there's a rescue dog at my feet and a rescue cat ignoring me from my favorite chair. I wouldn't have it any other way.

EXERCISE

Visit a Shelter

There are literally millions of animals—3.9 million dogs and 3.4 million cats alone—awaiting uncertain fates in shelters across the country. Right now.

Go pay your local shelter a visit and bring home one of these lovely creatures. Or go online to one of the many pet adoption sites.

If you're living in a place that doesn't allow pets, move.

Just kidding (sort of). You can always volunteer at the shelter or pet sit for a friend.

Until you make that move.

---| HAPPY PILLS |---

Pet a Puppy

"Whoever said you can't buy happiness forgot little puppies."
—Gene Hill

Just the act of petting a dog triggers the release of the happy hormones serotonin and oxytocin in our brains, according to a study by the University of Missouri-Columbia. What's more, petting a puppy also lowers levels of the unhappy stress hormone cortisol. A double whammy of good feelings.

The next time you need a shot of happy, don't reach for a happy pill. Reach for a happy pooch instead. Give her the sweet belly rub she's been waiting for and you'll both feel better in no time.

Take a Walk

"When I'm in turmoil, when I can't think, when I'm exhausted and afraid and feeling very, very alone, I go for walks…. I walk and I walk and sooner or later something comes to me, something to make me feel less like jumping off a building."
—Jim Butcher

YOU'VE HEARD THIS BEFORE, but here it is again: Few activities are as universally applauded for improving your mental, physical and emotional health as walking. Take a brisk half-hour walk every day and you'll not only feel happier, Mayo Clinic says you'll also find it easier to maintain a healthy weight, good balance and coordination; lower your risk of heart disease, high blood pressure and type 2 diabetes; and strengthen your bones and muscles.

For best results, you need to walk happy. That is, straighten your spine and swing your arms (as opposed to slumping along stiff-armed). Happy walking lifts your spirits.

When I suffered a terrible break-up several winters back,

I was a mess. The betrayal I felt was compounded by my anger at myself for being so gullible. After all, I was too old for this nonsense. What saved me was walking the dogs through the cranberry bogs in the snow every day. Walk and sigh, walk and cry, walk and rage. I walked off my sorrow one step at a time, and by spring, I was back among the living.

EXERCISE

The Road Less Traveled

Take a walk—but this time, walk somewhere new. This could mean just taking a different route through your neighborhood—but don't stop there. Try a walk in the next town over, or the next state or the next country.

Dream big walking dreams. Stroll along one of the world's most walkable nature paths or city streets. Here are a few to stoke your imagination:

- Rue Mouffetard in Paris's 5th arrondissement
- Great Ocean Walk in Australia
- The Freedom Trail in Boston
- Kamakura near Tokyo in Japan
- Central Park in New York City
- Old Man of Hoy on Orkney in Scotland
- The French Quarter in New Orleans
- Gordale Scar in the Yorkshire Dales in Britain
- Lombard Street in San Francisco's Russian Hill
- Provincetown Dunes on the Cape Cod National Seashore in Massachusetts

Staycation for One

"A vacation is having nothing to do
and all day to do it in."
—Robert Orben

WE'RE NOT GOOD AT GOING ON VACATION. More than
half of Americans will not take all their vacation this year,
mostly thanks to the mixed messages regarding time off that
permeate our corporate culture, according to a study by Oxford
Economics.

We know vacations are good for us; most managers agree
vacations help stave off burnout and are good for morale, not to
mention health and well-being.

The good news is, we don't have to go on vacation. We can
save money and our jobs by planning a staycation right at home.

Planning is the operative word here. Those of us who plan
our vacations take more time off and enjoy it more; we're
happier with our jobs, our relationships and our health and well-
being, as well as our vacations.

To enjoy a staycation as much as a traditional vacation, you have to make sure you've planned a real getaway—and not just from the office, but from the demands of domesticity at home as well. If you spend all your time off scrubbing floors and doing laundry, that's hardly a vacation.

So channel your favorite tour director and schedule your staycation activities—be they day hikes in the woods or concerts under the stars—ahead of time.

EXERCISE

Think Spa-cation

The trick to enjoying a staycation is to transform your home into a more spa-like environment. Here are some tips and tricks to creating an oasis right at home:

1. Have a cleaning service clean your house from top to bottom the day before your staycation begins.
2. Put away all timepieces, from clocks to watches.
3. Set your out-of-office automatic reply.
4. Stop your mail service temporarily and avoid the news.
5. Make a vacation playlist. And play it.
6. Light candles, burn incense, use essential oils.
7. Have your meals delivered.
8. Have a massage therapist make house calls.

Dine Out Solo

"For an adult, eating alone at
McDonald's is admitting a kind of defeat."
—Jonathan Carroll

WE EAT NEARLY HALF OF OUR MEALS alone these days—if you can even call them meals. According to the Hartman Group, meals are giving way to snacks, and family dinners are giving way to solo nibbles at our desks or in front of the TV. Our waistlines are none the better for it.

But it doesn't have to be that way. Eating alone is no reason to resort to Lean Cuisines or a handful of trail mix chowed down during reruns of *Big Brother*.

During one particularly challenging year, I was faced with eating supper alone—no folks, no kids, no significant other—on a regular basis for the first time in my life. I couldn't bear to cook for one, so I started training myself to dine alone. At the time I was living in Los Gatos, a posh little town I couldn't really afford nestled at the base of the Santa Cruz Mountains with lots of good restaurants. I picked one and went in. This was before iPhones, so I had no smartphone prop to disguise any discomfort I felt. But they treated me well at this lovely eatery, and I went back every Wednesday night. Now I travel for business a great deal and I welcome the opportunity to enjoy a fine meal on my own.

Dining out is one of the great pleasures of life. Learn to enjoy it, even (and especially) when you're on your own.

After all, you're in good company.

EXERCISE

Open Table for One

Pick one day of the week and make a dinner date with yourself. Choose somewhere new, somewhere you've always wanted to try. Do not take a book along; put away your phone.

Go for the full experience: Enjoy a pre-dinner cocktail, indulge in an appetizer and an entrée, linger over coffee and dessert. Take your time.

Not only will a leisurely meal help you enjoy your meal more, it will also lower your risk of obesity and heart disease, according to the American Heart Association.

Bon appétit!

Busy Hands, Happy Heart

"Split your own wood and it will warm you twice."
—Old New England saying

HANDIWORK IS AN OLD-FASHIONED WORD with 21st century appeal. Working with your hands—knitting, painting, origami, woodworking, gardening, cooking and similar activities—serves as an antidote to the toll technology is taking on our well-being.

We spend nearly 11 hours a day glued to our screens—smartphones, tablets, computers, TVs and more—according to an audience analysis by the Nielsen Company. And they say that number is rising as we speak, or rather, swipe.

But when we give ourselves the gift of time to bake a cake or plant a tree or play a guitar, not only do we experience the joy of creation and a sense of accomplishment, we also experience less stress, anxiety and depression, reports *Psychology Today*.

Working with our hands is also linked to peak performance and enhanced creativity.

So put that smartphone down and pick up a glue gun, crochet hook or a power drill. Use your hands to make something fun, something useful, something awesome. Something happy.

EXERCISE

Get Your Hands Dirty

On your next day off, plan to get your hands dirty. Commit to devoting a Saturday or Sunday or "Playing Hooky Day" to an activity that literally requires you to soil your hands with something other than the oil from your own fingerprints. Here's a list to choose from:

- Build a sandcastle
- Finger paint
- Tool some leather
- Sculpt something
- Brew some beer
- Work some metal
- Create a collage
- Build a model
- Weed a garden
- Build a snowman
- Dig a flower bed
- Pull a Jackson Pollock
- Make a sand painting
- Knead dough by hand

- Arrange flowers
- Refinish a table
- Rebuild an engine
- Build a robot
- Whittle something
- Throw a pot
- Wallpaper your guest room
- Reupholster a chair
- Make sushi
- Build a bookshelf
- Bind a book
- Make a pinewood derby car
- Make your own paper
- Découpage something

- Do a mosaic
- Make a stained glass window
- Paint clouds on the ceiling
- Write in calligraphy
- Tile your bathroom floor
- Make a picture frame
- Create your own essential oils

- Repair a toaster
- Stamp your own wrapping paper
- Stencil a border
- Decorate a cake
- Shoot and develop photographs
- Detail your car

If all else fails, hang out with a couple of toddlers and follow suit.
Practically everything they do gets their hands dirty.

Ritualize Your Homecoming

"You haven't really been anywhere
until you've got back home."
—Terry Pratchett

THE HARDEST PART OF LIVING ALONE may be coming
home to an empty house. That's when the reality of living alone
hits you hardest—and that reality is why adults are 80 percent
more likely to be depressed if they live alone, according to a
study in BMC Public Health.

But whether you're coming home to a studio apartment
or a mansion, a city flat or a cabin in the woods, you can make
that daily homecoming a welcoming experience—even when you
are only welcoming yourself.

This means not doing what most Americans do when they
get home: sit in front of the TV, watching/not watching

what's on as they multitask with electronic devices. Not a pretty picture—even without the apocryphal stained sweats and the day-old pizza—borne out by the Bureau of Labor Statistics' American Time Use Survey.

To make your hours of leisure more, well, leisurely, create a ritual that codifies what the comfort of home means to you. Such a ritual may mean that you:

Slip into something more comfortable (think silk pajamas, not sweats).

Pour yourself something good to drink (a glass of wine, an ice-cold beer, a cup of hot chocolate).

Make yourself a good meal and eat it off of pretty china. If you don't want to cook, stock up on good bread and cheese, fresh fruit and nuts, olives and crudités, smoked oysters and sardines, hummus and other dips.

Put on your favorite music—your choice!

Dance around the house, read a book, do some yoga, sit outside and watch the world go by—whatever feels like home to you.

EXERCISE

Bring Yourself Flowers

You are your first and last houseguest every day. Treat yourself the way you'd treat a houseguest. All the little niceties you welcome your guests with should be niceties you welcome yourself with as well. Come home to fresh flowers, clean linens, fluffy towels. Cookies in the cookie jar and bubble bath in the bathroom.

Make a list of the things you do to make your guests feel at home. Now do those things for yourself. Every. Single. One.

Treat Yourself

"Do not be afraid to give yourself
everything you've ever wanted in life."
—Frank Lloyd Wright

NO ONE KNOWS YOU BETTER THAN YOU DO.
Use that knowledge to indulge yourself in the ways that only
you would ever think to do. That's the gift of solitude;
it grants you the time and space you need to figure out who you
really are and what you really want. How you'd really most like
to spoil yourself.

Make a list of 100 treats for yourself. Yes, I said 100.
Such a significant number will force you to dig deep. Odds
are the longest gift list you've ever written for yourself before
is a Christmas list for Santa. It may be hard for you to come
up with things that are truly meaningful to you. Often these
are things that go beyond the bubble baths and glasses of wine
and good books to read, to big dreams that reflect your deepest
hopes and desires.

Think of this as a bucket list on steroids. Nine out of every 10 of us have made a bucket list, according to the *Journal of Palliative Medicine,* and the sooner we acknowledge and address the items on the list, the better. Too many of us wait too long to get started.

Get started.

EXERCISE

Start a Treat Jar

In that list of ways in which you'd like to treat yourself, there should be a couple of whoppers. That is, things that require more time, energy and resources than you may have right now—going back to school, climbing Mount Kilimanjaro, taking your mother on a trip to Las Vegas, you name it.

Choose one of those whoppers. Do the math. Put money in the jar toward that Whopper Treat every week. Make that dream a reality.

AROUND THE WORLD IN HAPPY WAYS

MONK FOR A DAY IN THE U.S.A.

Nothing says solitude more than a monastery. More and more people are (temporarily) abandoning the trials and tribulations of 21st century life for quiet contemplation at a monastery. According to Local Measure, monastery retreats for lay people are a growing trend in the travel business. Silent retreats are particularly popular, reports Lonely Planet. There are monasteries all around the United States, from ashrams and Zen centers to Trappist abbeys and Cistercian nunneries.

Be a monk for a day, a week, a year—and discover the joys of silence and solitude for yourself.

④
Happier Together

———

"There is only one happiness in this life,
to love and be loved."
—George Sand

———

Forget fame and fortune. The happiest people are those with the closest relationships. The quality of our relationships is the best predictor of whether we will live long and happy lives—better than social class, intelligence or even genes, according to a Harvard study.

If you're married, you're far more likely to be happy than your single, divorced or widowed peers, according to a study published in the *Journal of Health and Social Behavior*. If your spouse is your best friend, then you're doubly blessed—with twice as much well-being benefit, as reported in the *Journal of Happiness Studies*.

The trick is to maintain a warm and stable relationship. With nearly half of marriages ending in divorce, it's clear that happily ever after is harder than the fairy tales would have us believe.

But the rewards are worth it. A loving relationship pays off—in happiness, well-being, good health and even longevity. In this section, we'll explore the ways in which we can be happier together, every day of our lives.

Practice Compassion

"If you want others to be happy, practice compassion.
If you want to be happy, practice compassion."
—Dalai Lama XIV

THE DALAI LAMA (and probably your mother) is right: It is better to give than receive—and it will make you happier. Do something nice for your significant other and you'll be happier for it, according to a study in the journal *Emotion*. This holds true even when your thoughtful gesture goes unacknowledged.

The best relationships are those in which both parties practice these small random acts of kindness for one another, without keeping score and without expecting anything in return. (That last part is the tricky part, as anyone who's even been divorced can tell you. Once you start keeping score, it's the beginning of the end.)

This is not about spending a lot of money—which only works if what you're spending it on is not simply meant to impress but actually benefit your spouse—it's about attention and affection. It's the little things: holding hands while you walk down the street, agreeing to change your plans to accommodate your partner's (rather than the other way around), biting your tongue the next time you're tempted to criticize.

Every moment together is an opportunity to practice compassion. Take advantage of this opportunity. The more you do, the happier you'll be...together.

EXERCISE

The List of Compassion

Paying attention is the key. When you first fall in love, you don't miss anything. You're so focused on one another that you can't help but see a million ways to please each other every day. But as time goes by and you settle into a routine, this hyper-awareness fades.

For the next 24 hours, pay attention to your beloved. Make a note of every opportunity that arises during the course of the day where you could do something compassionate—and do it.

Forgive

"There is no love without forgiveness,
and there is no forgiveness without love."
—Bryant H. McGill

FORGIVE US OUR TRESPASSES. Forgive and forget. To err is human; to forgive, divine.

Forgiveness is one of those virtues most lauded by our spiritual heroes—from Jesus and the Buddha to Mother Teresa and Gandhi—and most ignored by the rest of us. Maybe because it's just so darn hard.

But our happiness ultimately depends on our ability to forgive those who trespass against us. Couples who are able to forgive each other have happier and longer-lasting relationships, according to a study in the *Journal of Family Psychology*. Forgiving couples are better at resolving conflict and at reaching compromises than their unforgiving peers. They're less apt to hold grudges and nurse resentments or treat each other meanly. Not only do they forgive each other's failings, but they forgive themselves their own. One last bonus: Forgiving couples live longer, according to a study in the *Journal of Behavioral Medicine.*

Forgiveness is a powerful force. When I reconciled with my second ex-husband more than a decade later, our families were incredulous. When my sister-in-law asked how on earth we could come back together when we couldn't even be in the same room together for years, Michael said: "It's amazing what a little forgiveness can do."

Amen.

EXERCISE

Water Under the Bridge

What's the hardest thing you must forgive your partner for? Write it down on a dry leaf.

What's the hardest thing you have to forgive yourself for? Write that down on a leaf, too.

Stick them in your pocket.

Drive to the nearest bridge traversing a creek, stream or river, one where you can safely park and walk along the structure from one side to another. Walk halfway across; stop there. Pull out the leaf on which you've written your significant other's transgression and toss it over the bridge. Watch it as it floats down to the water below, flowing under the bridge and beyond. When it's out of sight, continue to the opposite bank. Now proceed back along the bridge, stopping again at the halfway mark. Pull the leaf naming your transgression from your pocket. Throw it over the side. Watch it fall, only to be swept along with the current.

Water under the bridge.

╌ HAPPY PILLS ╌

Bad Cop Cortisol, Good Cop Oxytocin

"Revenge, at first though sweet,
Bitter ere long back on itself recoils."
—John Milton

Holding a grudge is toxic. Not just for your relationship, but for your body. Feelings of anger, bitterness and vengefulness raise your blood pressure and trigger the fight or flight response, flooding your cells with the stress hormone known as cortisol. Too much stress equals too much cortisol—and can lead to anxiety, depression, weight gain, insomnia, headaches, digestive issues, heart disease and memory and focus problems.

Given how bad excess cortisol is for you, nursing your grudges is in effect a form of self-sabotage. But it doesn't have to be that way. Letting go of your resentments and learning to resolve conflicts amicably can reverse this process, boosting levels of the feel-good hormone, oxytocin.

Bad cop, good cop: That's why it's in your own best interest to forgive and forget.

Play Together

"The idea that couples that play together stay
together is very true. Like all good things,
it takes planning and creativity."
—Nina Atwood

COUPLES WHO PLAY TOGETHER, stay together.
Playing together—and by that we mean trying out new and
fun things as a couple—brings you closer together,
creates happy memories and enhances your positive feelings
about one another and your relationship, according to a
study published in the *Journal of Personality and Social
Psychology.* You'll be a happier couple, and it's the happier
couples who stay together.

What's more, doing novel and enjoyable activities together
can help counteract the boredom that ultimately dooms many
relationships. The next time you're just sitting around the
house, you at one end of the couch and your partner on the
other, respective phones in hand, pocket those phones and go
do something engaging and entertaining. If you can't think

of anything, share a bottle of wine and come up with a list together—now that'll be fun.

EXERCISE

Play Harder

There's fun, and then there's sports. Couples who get fit together keep their relationship in good shape as well. They feel stronger and more attractive—and they stay together longer, according to a study in the *Journal of Sports Medicine and Physical Fitness*.

The best part: Exercising together boosts the libido for both sexes, and that post-workout glow of endorphins spells more energy for more playing around later.

Play outside and you'll have even more fun. Golf, riding, tennis and yoga can all help couples build trust, show more affection and fight less often.

Make an exercise date with your significant other every week. For best results, choose a sport you both enjoy and that won't bring out the über-competitor in either of you. It's supposed to be fun.

Appreciate One Another

"Appreciation is a wonderful thing. It makes what is excellent in others belong to us as well."
—Voltaire

WHAT DO YOU MOST appreciate about your partner? Name at least three things. Right now.

Here's a cheat sheet:

- Sense of humor
- Perseverance
- Thoughtfulness
- Optimism
- Creativity
- Loyalty
- Discipline
- Determination

- Confidence
- Patience
- Enthusiasm
- Respectfulness
- Trustworthiness
- Honesty
- Adaptability

Noticing and acknowledging each other's good points is one of the best things you can do for your relationship—and yourself. Appreciation is a two-way street: Feeling good about what's good about your beloved makes you feel good about yourself, too.

In a George Mason University study, the couples who most appreciated one another's strengths enjoyed more fulfilling and committed relationships and more satisfying sex lives. They felt supported by their partners, in their goals as well as their personal growth.

EXERCISE

Seven Days of Appreciation

Appreciation may be one of the most overlooked aspects of happiness. But it doesn't have to be that way. Appreciation is just an observation away. Pay attention, and appreciation grows.

Remember those three things you most appreciate about your significant other? Write them down. Ask yourself when you last expressed your admiration for those fine qualities.

Vow to compliment your partner every day, one way or another, for one week. This can be as modest as a simple thank you for being you, or as grand as a pricey thank you gift for going above and beyond.

Celebrate Your Differences

"The reason as to why we are
attracted to our opposites is
because they are our salvation from
the burden of being ourselves."
—Kamand Kojouri

OPPOSITES ATTRACT—that's the conventional wisdom,
and that's what most of us believe. At least, according to the
same studies that tell us the most successful relationships
are between those who are more like each other in terms
of background, socioeconomic status, values and physical
attractiveness. Yet in terms of personality, opposites do
attract—and may be happier together, according to a Prepare/
Enrich study. Findings suggest couples with complementary
personalities—not similar personalities—are happiest.

Celebrating our differences means seeing them as
complementary, rather than polar opposites. It means finding

ways to "enhance or emphasize the qualities of each other," rather than letting our differences come between us.

Because opposites do attract, and that can make all the difference.

EXERCISE

The Compromise of Opposites

Our disagreements are often rooted in our differences. Fights about money, because you're thrifty and your partner is not. Fights about sex, because you're in the mood and your partner is not. Fights about parenting, because you're strict and your partner is not.

My second husband and I fought a lot about parties when we were first married. He hated them; I loved them. Now, decades later, we have come to an understanding. A compromise of sorts. I still love parties and still go to parties. He still hates parties and only accompanies me when we know two of our favorite couples will also be there. If he wants to leave early, he goes out to his truck and takes a nap until I'm ready to leave. The bonus: When the weather is bad, he'll drive me to the event anyway because he's a much better driver than I am and he worries about me. Even if the aforementioned favorite couple friends will not be there and even if that means he sleeps in the truck. I get my party, and he gets his forty winks.

Think about what you argue about most. Now come up with a compromise that suits you both. Try it on for size the next time that issue raises its ugly head. And watch beast become beauty.

Honor Your Boundaries

"Every human being must have boundaries
in order to have successful relationships or a successful
performance in life."
—Henry Cloud

THE URGE TO MERGE—isn't that what love is all about?
Yet the happiest couples are the ones who set boundaries for
themselves and honor those boundaries. This is true for the
same reason being with friends often makes people happier than
being with family—friends tend to be better at respecting us
and honoring our boundaries. According to a *Mappiness* survey,
being with friends boosts our mood by 8.2 percent, more than
being with partners, which boosts moods by 5.9 percent; other
family members, 2.9 percent; and children, 1.4 percent. The
survey tracked 50,000 people as they interacted some 3 million
times with others, and they rated those interactions in terms of
how happy and relaxed they felt during them.

The results stunned some participants, but we already know that couples who view each other as best friends are happier, and friends don't let friends lower their boundaries.

EXERCISE

Limit Two

While it's important for you and your significant other to set boundaries and honor them, it's equally important that you set boundaries for yourselves as a couple too. Couples without agreed-upon boundaries risk an erosion of commitment over time—an erosion that can lead to trouble later on. According to a study by the Relationship Institute at UCLA, the greater the level of commitment, the better the odds of a marriage lasting.

Not particularly surprising, but what might surprise you is how social media may be breaching your boundaries as a couple—and how deleterious an effect it can have. In a study conducted by Pew Research Center, nearly half of millennials admitted their social media activities had an impact on their relationships.

From oversharing aspects of your life together to snooping on each other or worse, social media can be tough on your relationship. Put your electronic devices away and sit down together and talk about the way you use social media. Work out some boundaries you can agree on as a couple.

Note: If you're not on social media—at least not enough to endanger your relationship—congratulate yourselves with some electronics-free time alone together in bed. You earned it.

Communicate

"We have two ears and one mouth so that we can
listen twice as much as we speak."
—Epictetus

I KNOW, I KNOW, we've all heard this a million times
before. We've watched all the TV psychologists on talk shows
lauding the benefits of communication, read all the
relationship books lauding the benefits of communication,
processed all the studies (and studies and studies) lauding the
benefits of communication.

And still, according to a poll from lifestyle site Your
Tango, communication issues are the biggest reason people
get divorced (followed by a failure to resolve conflict, which is
hard to do when you don't, you know, communicate). Men cite
their partners' nagging and complaining as the biggest irritants.
Women cite their partners' refusal to validate their opinions and
feelings as the biggest irritants.

And so it goes.

But it doesn't have to be that way. We can learn to talk

to each other about anything—money, sex, secrets and other hot-button topics—and when we do, we help make our relationship bulletproof.

What's the hardest thing for you to talk about with your partner? If you're not sure, ask yourself which topic you avoid talking about the most. Think about why that is and what you might do about it.

EXERCISE

Talk it Out

Choose a time when you can be alone with your significant other with no interruptions. Pick a good day, when both of you are calm and relaxed and unhurried. Light candles and get comfortable. Now take a scrap of paper and write down the one thing you love most about your relationship while your partner does the same, folding the papers once you've finished. Exchange the folded pieces of paper.

Talk about it. Take turns. If one of you is a big talker and the other is not, let the less communicative of you go first.

Then switch papers and talk again. Be sure to listen as much as you talk.

Try this exercise once a week and eventually move on to things about your relationship that you don't like so much. Remember to talk and to listen.

Trust

—

"The best proof of love is trust."
—Joyce Brothers

—

IF YOU WANT TO BE A HAPPY COUPLE, ground your relationship in trust. That may sound obvious, but a surprising number of couples trust each other so little that they snoop on each other. One in three women rummage through their husband's cell phones, while twice as many of their husbands are rummaging through theirs, according to a study reported by CNN. Nine percent of women also check their husband's social media accounts, while 3 percent of their husbands are checking theirs, as reported in a study from OnePoll.

Yet trust is integral to fulfilling relationships. Trusting people releases oxytocin, the feel-good hormone that we've talked about before. When you trust somebody, you literally feel better physically and emotionally. What's more, oxytocin itself has been found to increase trust and social bonding—creating a happy loop of good feelings—according to a study reported in *The New York Times.*

If you're thinking, well, that only lasts until your partner hurts you by breaking that trust, you have a point. But that cynicism comes at a cost, according to a study from Northwestern University and Redeemer University College. The more trusting you are—whether that trust proves unfounded or not—the happier you'll be with yourself and your relationships. Trust translates to optimism, collaboration and the ability to let go of resentments—all critical aspects of maintaining trust. Not to mention that lovely oxytocin rush.

Let trust begin with you. Trust your partner to do the right thing by you and by your relationship. Granted, the more trustworthy you are, the greater your fear of being disappointed or hurt when someone fails to live up to that trust. But not trusting people is a recipe for unhappiness, both in yourself and in your relationships.

Do you trust your spouse? How does that trust manifest itself? Have you crossed the line when it comes to financial fidelity, sexual fidelity or emotional fidelity? Be as hard on yourself as you are on your partner. If you think you are, think again: Study after study reveals that the same behavior we condemn in others we often excuse in ourselves. (Snooping comes to mind.)

The best way to stop the erosion of trust is to talk about it. Sit down with your partner and have a "trust chat." Talk about the things that worry you both. And don't be afraid to tell the truth.

EXERCISE

Tell No Lies

Honest people are happier and healthier. A study from the University of Notre Dame found that people who strove to tell the truth more often—meaning they told fewer lies, large and small—for 10 weeks reported better physical and mental health as a result. Whether they resisted telling white lies or major lies didn't matter, participants felt better physically and emotionally regardless.

For the next 24 hours, pledge to tell the truth to everyone, especially your partner. Remember: Lies of omission are still lies. Tell the truth, the whole truth and nothing but the truth for one day. And see what happens.

Be Passionate

———

"And yet another moral occurs to me now:
Make love when you can. It's good for you."
—Kurt Vonnegut

———

SEX IS VITAL to the health of any intimate relationship. Good sex not only makes you happier, it makes you healthier, so much so you'll actually live longer if you do it often enough.

How much sex is happy sex? According to the Archives of Sexual Behavior, most of us have sex 54 times a year—around once a week. And there's a reason for that: Study after study confirms having sex once a week is the baseline for closeness. There's nothing wrong with having sex more often—lucky you!— but sex once a week is what you need to keep your relationship close and connected. A study reported in *Social Psychological and Personality Science* tracked 30,000 Americans over more than 40 years, and the findings bear this out: The happiest couples have sex once a week. Couples who fool around more often are no happier than those who have sex once a week—but those who do it less than once a week are also less happy.

So closely intertwined are sex and your happiness as a couple that if you go from monthly sex to weekly sex, you'll experience a leap in happiness equivalent to making an extra $50,000 a year, according to a National Bureau of Economic Research study. Fifty grand's worth of happiness just for having more sex—what's not to like?

EXERCISE

The Talk

If you're not having sex—or you're having bad sex—then it's time to do something about it. The better the sex, the happier you are, according to a study conducted by Australia's Monash University. For men, that boost in happiness tends to be more related to the physical aspects of sex, and for women, the emotional aspects. Either way, you owe it to yourself and your relationship to have good sex at least once a week.

If you aren't having sex, ask yourself why not. Sit down and have The Talk. Figure it out. There are many reasons couples fall into sexless patterns: too much stress, not enough sleep, low self-esteem, bad body image, medical issues and even smart devices. Put away your electronics and focus on one another.

If you're having bad sex, ask yourself what's wrong with it. It's not rocket science: you know what pleases you and you know what pleases your partner. If you don't, it's time for a little experimentation and exploration.

If it's just a question of time, get a babysitter, go off for the weekend, turn off the TV and turn on a little Sade. Give each other a massage. Please yourself—and let your partner come along for the ride. Whatever floats your boat.

Just do it.

Be Affectionate

"Affection is responsible for nine-tenths of whatever solid
and durable happiness there is in our lives."
—C.S. Lewis

AS WE'VE SEEN, couples who have more sex are happier. But
it's not only the orgasm itself—and all those feel-good hormones
that go with it—that makes us happier. The cuddling afterward
is just as important to our happiness and releases feel-good
hormones as well.

After we have sex, we feel more positive, according to
Psychology Today. When we feel more positive, we are more
affectionate and we have more sex. And so on and so on and so
on. This lovely continuous repeating cycle of sex, positivity and
affection spells more happiness all around.

Even better: This positivity has a long tail, with couples
reporting greater satisfaction with their relationship up to six
months later. All this for sex and affection once a week.

All kinds of affection—hugging, kissing, holding hands,
touching, cuddling—leave positive effects on our relationships.

Be affectionate, and you are 47 percent more likely to feel close to family members; ditto for those who are affectionate with you. Even when you touch someone subliminally—subliminal touching defined as when you touch people so subtly that it escapes their conscious awareness—you dramatically boost their positive feelings, not just about you but about themselves.

Years ago, I fell in love with a lovely guy. During that first intense getting-to-know-you period of our relationship, we went out to breakfast on a beautiful Sunday morning. Filled with happiness, I leaned over and touched his face. He was stunned. No one had ever touched his face that way before. He was very moved. And he touched mine.

Affection: It's as simple as a touch.

EXERCISE

A Jar of Affection

Are you affectionate by nature? Even if you are, you may need a reminder to express that affection more often with your partner. If you're not affectionate by nature, you need to practice.

One of my favorite things is when I'm washing dishes at the sink and my guy comes up behind me and puts his arms around me. There's something so intimate and homey and heartwarming in that gesture. It makes me feel so good.

Draw up a list of the small tokens of affection that you love, and the ones you know your partner loves: hugs, kisses, holding hands, etc. Write each one down on a separate scrap of paper.

Put them in a jar. Pull one out every morning and make it your gesture of affection for the day. Begin with your partner, but don't stop there. Everybody needs a hug now and then—kids, colleagues, family, friends. Spread the love!

Relax

"Slow down and everything you are chasing will come
around and catch you."
—John De Paola

THE HAPPIEST COUPLES are relaxed with one another. They chill out together. They hang out together. They know how to do nothing together. They live longer, more satisfying lives.

Stressed couples are not happy. Stressed couples fight more and have less sex. They do not live longer, more satisfying lives. In fact, the stress of an unhappy marriage is as bad for you as smoking and insufficient physical activity. It triples the risk of heart surgery, heart attacks and death, according to an American Medical Association study. Unhappy couples also have lower immunity, more inflammation and are slower to heal.

As bad as marital stress is for men, it's even worse for women, who suffer higher blood pressure, higher cholesterol, higher body mass indexes, depression, anxiety and anger.

Relaxed couples are happier couples, both in their relationships and in life in general. If you're bringing stress home with you from your job—and up to 40 percent of us are—that's all the more reason to find a way to relax together. Your job stress affects your partner as well as yourself, according to the *Wall Street Journal*. Be happy and relaxed together. Do what you need to do to chill out.

EXERCISE

Chill Night

Forget date night. What stressed-out couples really need is a chill night. Find some activity that you can do together, one you both find relaxing. Not only will you lower your stress levels, you'll be happier as a couple, according to the *Journal of Social and Personal Relationships*.

My husband and I like to kayak with our dog. Between the lake and the dog and the sweet slap of the oars in the water, it's a lovely meditative way to hang out together. Before kayaking, we'd never been particularly physically active together; we always went our separate ways when it came to sports and physical exercise. But finding something we both love to do has made all the difference.

Every couple should find something to do together. Whether it's walking in the woods or hiking up a mountain, bicycling along the coast or playing tennis, bowling or binge-watching HBO, whatever you like to do together that relaxes and rejuvenates you both is good for your relationship—and for you.

Be Open

"Only someone who is ready for everything, who doesn't exclude any experience, even the most incomprehensible, will live the relationship with another person as something alive and will himself sound the depths of his own being."
—Rainer Maria Rilke

BEING OPEN TO NEW EXPERIENCES and different ways of thinking and doing is critical to maintaining a strong connection with your partner in the long term. People change over time, and along with those changes come new challenges. Every stage of married life has its delights and demands, from the giddy intensity of first love and the early accommodations of moving in together to the cheerful chaos of raising a family and the sudden solitude of the empty nest. Surviving and thriving for the long haul requires an adaptability born of openness and receptivity. That's why the happiest married couples are not the newlyweds, as you might think, but the couples celebrating their 20-year anniversaries and beyond, according to a joint

Pennsylvania State and Brigham Young University study. The longer a couple is married, the more time they tend to spend together. They appreciate one another more and enjoy each other's company more. The happiest couples describe one another as emotionally intelligent, and that emotional intelligence allows them to approach their relationship with open minds and hearts, receptive to each other's views and ideas and ways of doing things.

Of course, you don't have to wait 20 years to be happier together. You can learn to be more open and receptive and tuned in to each other. Starting now.

EXERCISE

Trading Places

Sometimes the smallest things can irritate us—a few angry words and before you know it, you're in the middle of a big argument. Think about the recurring disagreements that affect your relationship: the fight you have before every party, the inevitable Saturday morning clash over chores, the endless quarrel over disciplining the dog.

Write down all the things your partner would say during one of these petty squabbles. Now have your partner write down all the things you would say in rebuttal. Exchange lists; play each other's roles. Laugh at how ridiculous you both sound. Brainstorm solutions.

┤ AROUND THE WORLD IN HAPPY WAYS ├

THE LANGUAGES OF LOVE

While some aspects of love are universal, when it comes to love and marriage, each culture has its own unique traditions. Nowhere is this more apparent than in the very language used to describe being happier together:

- *Cwtch,* a Welsh word meaning safe haven, roughly translated as "hug."
- *Forelsket,* a Norwegian expression describing the special euphoria you feel when you first fall in love.
- *Iktsuarpok,* an Inuit word for the excitement you feel when you're waiting for someone to show up at your house.
- *Viraag,* a Hindi expression for the heartache you suffer when you're away from your beloved.
- *Oodal,* a Tamil word describing the phony pout you put on after bickering with your lover.
- *Cafuné,* a Brazilian Portuguese expression for running your fingers through your sweetheart's hair.
- *Ya'aburnee,* an Arabic word roughly translated as "you bury me," that desire that you will die first so you never have to live without your beloved.

(5)

Happier
Body

———

"And your very flesh shall be a great poem."
—Walt Whitman

———

Your body is a temple. Take care of your body and your body will take care of you. Your body is the only place you have to live. The aphorisms go on and on, yet a surprising number of us do not take good care of our bodies. According to a CDC U.S. National Health and Nutrition Survey, a whopping 97.3 percent of Americans do not lead a completely healthy lifestyle—a healthy lifestyle defined as one in which we exercise moderately, eat sensibly, maintain a healthy weight and do not smoke. Nothing earthshaking. Nothing undoable. Nothing we haven't heard before.

Healthy bodies are happy bodies. And when our bodies are not happy, they tell us in no uncertain terms. They make it perfectly clear—we have the aches and pains and discomfort and disease to prove it. Our physical well-being is not all that suffers; when we are ill, our risk of depression increases—and the more serious the illness, the greater the risk. One in 3 people with a chronic illness will suffer serious depression as well—and depending on the illness, that risk can run even higher, according to *WebMD*. For example, those who endure chronic pain run a 54 percent risk of depression; for those who suffer a heart attack, the risk runs as high as 65 percent.

The moral of this story: A healthy body is a happy body is a happier you. The time is now.

Stretch

"Yoga is the fountain of youth.
You're only as young as your spine is flexible."
—Bob Harper

OUR BODIES WERE MADE TO STRETCH. Watch a baby reach for her toes, a toddler pull himself up out of his play yard, a child cartwheeling and handstanding and somersaulting across the lawn.

But as we get older, we tighten up—and not in a good way. We forget to stretch. Stretching is particularly important if you suffer back pain, which is the most common disability in the world. More than 80 percent of Americans alone suffer back pain—often caused by too much sitting, the worst culprit when it comes to back pain, according to the American Physical Therapy Association. When I discovered yoga, I felt as if I had discovered the fountain of youth. I'd go into every class feeling every bit the middle-aged woman I was, and come out feeling like I was 26 all over again. (And if feeling like you're 26 again isn't happiness, I don't know what is.)

I'd forgotten how good it felt to walk around in a young healthy body, but yoga was helping me to remember. I started off barely able to touch my toes, but over time I could place my broad palms flat on the floor, twist my stiff writer's arms into eagle pose, even pull my aging legs into a full lotus position. Best of all, the chronic shoulder, neck and back pain I'd suffered since I'd injured my neck as a child completely disappeared (and only returns when I spend too much time hunched over my laptop and too little time on my mat).

That's the power of a good stretch.

EXERCISE

Say Om

Once I realized how good yoga made me feel, I wanted to know why it worked. I wanted to know why I felt decades younger after every class, why I slept better at night, why I had more energy and less neck/back/shoulder pain. Even why I'd lost 30 pounds in a year—and gained some of it back whenever I failed to practice regularly enough. That's when I decided to do my yoga teacher training—so I could learn the science and the philosophy of the practice that was making such a difference in my life.

What I learned was that stretching your body is just the beginning. All that time on the mat helped me stretch myself in myriad ways, not only taking on physical challenges—learning to stand on my head at 54!— but taking on mental and emotional challenges as well, from writing my first mystery novel to reconciling with my (second) ex-husband.

How can you stretch yourself? Start with a yoga class and see where it takes you. Your inner 26-year-old will be glad you did.

Balance

"Be strong then, and enter into your own body;
there you have a solid place for your feet."
—Kabir

READY, STEADY, GO. That's what balance is all about. From the time we manage to toddle across the room under our own power, on our own two feet, we take our ability to navigate the world of streets and sidewalks, steps and stairs and cobblestones for granted. We may even push the boundaries of balance, dancing in toe shoes and prancing on balance beams and hurtling across the ice after a puck.

And then the next thing you know, we grow up and the only thing we can balance is our checkbook. As we age, our balance and coordination may fail us. Death rates due to falling are up an astonishing 30 percent among older adults over the past decade, according to the CDC. If this trend continues, that will mean seven deaths from a fall every hour by 2030.

The good news is you can rebalance your body—and your life. Both yoga and tai chi can help you improve your balance and coordination, no matter your age.

EXERCISE

Balancing Act

When I was doing my yoga teacher training, I was spectacularly bad at balance poses. I could do most anything with both of my two feet or my one big butt firmly on the ground, but ask me to balance on one leg or kneel on one knee or stand on my head and I tottered every time. "What is out of balance in your life?" Michelle, my yoga teacher trainer, would always ask me with a smile.

I hated that question. Mostly because the answer at the time in my life was "everything." With my kids all grown and gone and my career in free fall and my love life nonexistent, I was off-balance in virtually every way. Still, I rejected Michelle's all-too-literal interpretation of my trouble with balance poses. I need to work on my coordination and concentration, practice my spotting, overcome my fear of being upside down. All of which I did—at the same time I was recalibrating my work/life balance for the better.

Chicken or the egg? Ask yourself what's out of balance in your life—and then try that tree pose again.

Exercise

———

"Physical fitness is not only one of the
most important keys to a healthy body, it is the basis
of dynamic and creative intellectual activity."
—John F. Kennedy

———

WE ALL KNOW WE'RE SUPPOSED TO EXERCISE.
This is not news. We all know how good exercise is for us—
mind, body and spirit. And that's not news either. The exercise
experts may change their minds about how much or how
often or how intense, but the bottom line is this: You have
to exercise.

Your body needs it the way it needs air and food and
sleep (and yes, we'll get to those). The trick is to find something
you like to do and keep on doing it regularly. Over the years,
my exercise routine has changed from ballet to jogging to
aerobics to boxing and now finally to yoga. Yoga is my favorite...
right now.

As your body, interests and life change, your exercise
changes. I have dogs who need exercise. And grandkids who like

to play. And I live in a big old house in New England with lots of stairs and a garden to weed and leaves to rake and snow to shovel. All of that counts.

Here's a list of some things you can do to make sure you incorporate exercise into your life:

1. Get (or borrow) a dog. If you have any heart at all, you'll find it impossible to resist how excited they get at the prospect of a walk or a visit to the dog park. People with dogs walk 22 more minutes a day than people without dogs, according to a study published in *BMC Public Health*.

2. Have (or babysit) a kid. When my kids were little, we lived near the beach. We ran through the sand and built sandcastles, we played beach volleyball and tossed around a Frisbee on the beach. Now I have grandkids who like to hike, so I hike. They like to swim, so I swim. They like to skate, so I skate. I even crawl on my stomach through caves because they like crawling on their stomachs through caves. Anything for the grandkids.

3. Become friends with people who move. The more active your peers are, the more active you are likely to be. (This is true for our kids, too, who are more active when their friends are, according to a *Journal of Pediatric Psychology* study.) Michael and I like to kayak, and we like to walk with the dogs through the woods. With my friend Michele, I go to yoga. With my friend

Michaela, I go dancing. And with my kids and grandkids,
I just try to keep up.

You don't have to be Serena Williams, you just have to go
for a walk 30 minutes every day. Even if it's just up and down
the stairs or around the block or on your exercise bike or your
treadmill. All that matters is that you do it. And keep on doing it.

EXERCISE

Five Every 30

Get up off your ass. It's really that simple. Sitting is the new smoking
and it's killing us. The more you sit, the greater your risk of dying young,
according to a study in the *Annals of Internal Medicine*. But get up and
move around every half hour and that risk drops. People who sit less than
30 minutes at a time are the least likely to die early.

My smartwatch tells me when I've been sitting too long. It beeps at
me, and I get up. I dance, I jump, I jog in place, I do a down dog or a plank
or a forward fold. Five minutes is all I need.

Set your watch or alarm clock or egg timer to alert you every 30
minutes. Start now. Get off that couch, shut your door and move.

Sleep

"I love sleep because it is both pleasant
and safe to use. Pleasant because one is in the best
possible company, and safe because sleep is the
consummate protection against the unseemliness that
Is the invariable consequence of being awake."
—Fran Lebowitz

I LOVE TO SLEEP. I can sleep anywhere, anytime. Like Fran
Lebowitz, I think of sleep as a hobby I can't live without.
I rely on a good night's sleep every night so much I can't
imagine trying to function without it (and the only time I had
to, when my first child was an infant, remains a weary blur).
Yet 80 million Americans are sleep-deprived, and therefore at
a higher risk for heart disease, diabetes, obesity, stroke, high
blood pressure and depression, according to the American
Psychological Association. Lose sleep and odds are your work
and relationships will suffer—you even have a greater risk of
crashing your car. Whatever you do, stop priding yourself on
getting by on so little sleep. It's not a badge of honor,

it's a death sentence.

If you have trouble sleeping, try meditation, exercise and fresh air. Avoid caffeine late at night, ditto for big meals. Make sure you're sleeping on a decent bed. Do whatever you have to do to get the sleep you need. I used to sleep 10 hours a night as a young woman; now that I'm older I do fine on seven to eight hours, which is what the APA recommends for optimal health. Do your body a favor: Go to bed.

EXERCISE

Bath, Book, Bed

When the kids were little I never had trouble getting to sleep. My firstborn—who never wanted sleep because she never wanted to miss anything—taught me the hard way that I needed to enforce bedtime. Because everyone in the family needed a good night's sleep.

So we established a ritual: bath, book, bed. I'd give my kids a bath, then I'd read them a book and tuck them into bed. At first, of course, I read to them; when they were old enough I'd read a page and then they'd read a page. Then they went to bed. Lights out. Shut the door. End of story.

Create a bedtime ritual for yourself. Bath, book, bed still works pretty well, at least for me. Give it a try. Sweet dreams.

Note: If you do read at night, make sure you read a printed book. Or if you're reading on your tablet, make sure you switch the light setting from cool to warm. According to a Harvard Medical School report, blue light at night will affect your circadian rhythm and mess with your sleep cycles, which can raise the risk of cancer, diabetes and heart disease. It can even make you fat.

Stop

———

"Rest is not idleness, and to lie on the grass under trees on a summer's day, listening to the murmur of the water, or watching the clouds float across the sky, is by no means a waste of time."
—John Lubbock

———

ONE DAY DURING my yoga teacher training, our trainer, Michelle, came up to me in class and patted my cheeks. "Now these are some good adrenal glands. You must be very good at doing nothing."

Your adrenal glands secrete adrenaline whenever your fight-or-flight response is triggered. All that adrenaline is great when you're running from a saber-toothed tiger, but when you're just sitting at your computer worrying about work or driving home frustrated by rush-hour traffic or up all night stressing out over unpaid bills, that same adrenaline is too much too soon. Like revving your engine over and over again when you've got nowhere to go. You flood your engine and it shuts down.

When your adrenal glands are exhausted—known as adrenal fatigue—you are exhausted too. And you look it. Chill out and give your adrenal glands a rest. Not only will you feel better, you'll look better.

Michelle was right. I work very hard, but I'm also an expert in doing absolutely nothing.

When I get stressed out, I stop. I read or sleep or do a little yoga or watch reruns of *Bones*. I'm particularly good at looking out the windows of my home office, watching the trees and the squirrels and the chipmunks and the hawks and the wild turkeys.

You, too, can learn to be good at doing nothing. The next time you find yourself running, running, running, just stop. Take a minute, take a deep breath. Curl up on the couch, close your eyes, take a nap. Just stop.

EXERCISE

Stoplight

Set your alarm to STOP twice a day. Try to schedule these stops at the times of day when you feel the most drained or exhausted or frazzled: mid-morning, mid-afternoon, right before quitting time. Set those alarms for those times and when the alarm goes off, STOP.

Even if all you do is hide out in the bathroom from your kids, your boss or your significant other, you can close your eyes and breathe in and out for 10 minutes. You can do nothing—and do it well.

Programming these little stops right into your day can help you learn to do nothing and beat adrenal fatigue. You can even try one of the relaxation apps, such as *Buddhify*, *Calm* or *Headspace*.

Look

"To lose confidence in one's body
is to lose confidence in oneself."
—Simone de Beauvoir

TAKE A LONG HARD look at your body. Embrace it.
No more fat-shaming, no more body-shaming, no more shaming
at all. This glorious body of yours has taken you this far for
better or for worse. And odds are it's treated you a lot better
than you've treated it.

Happiness is feeling good about your body. Feel good
about the way you look, and you're likely to feel good about
your life, your significant other, your sex life, your family, your
finances and yourself, according to a recent survey by Chapman
University.

Learning to love your body means bucking the airbrushed
perfection bill of goods we're being sold in this culture. And buck
it we must. When my daughter was only 10 years old, she said to
me, "I have a big butt like you, Mom. It's terrible to have a big
butt. It's ugly."

Now this was long before Jennifer Lopez and the Kardashians made big butts a thing. I knew what my daughter was talking about; I'd come of age—big butt and all—in the hipless Twiggy era. Still, I was fine with my own derriere; I came from a long line of women with ample hips. "Welcome to the big butt club," I told my daughter.

Love your body as it is. Welcome to the big butt club or the small boob club or the thinning hair club: whatever club you belong to, celebrate it.

EXERCISE

Love Letter to Your Body

Write a love letter to your own sweet self. Make a list of all the things you like about your body: your perfect little ears, your dimpled knees, your broad shoulders.

If you can't think of anything, consider these: The two feet that have carried you since the day you were born. The hands that have chopped vegetables and fixed engines and typed reports and plaited hair and built shelves and knitted scarves and held babies and hugged friends and petted puppies. The legs that keep you upright, stride you down the street and up the stairs. The arms that carry kids, groceries, firewood. The neck that holds your head up where it belongs. The heart that keeps on beating and the eyes that keep on seeing and the ears that keep on hearing. Every part of your body that works 24/7 just to keep you alive. Write it all down.

Yours is a beautiful body so look at it—and appreciate it. Appreciate that body and love it as it is now.

And strive to be nicer to it.

Listen to Your Body

"Our own body is the best health system we have—
if we know how to listen to it."
—Christiane Northrup

YOUR BODY WILL SPEAK TO YOU—if you're listening.
The ache in your lower back when you carry the groceries, the
twinges in your knees when you lift yourself up off the couch,
the heavy breathing when you climb the stairs.

Listening is how you check in with your body. How often do
you do that? You take your car in for a checkup and an oil change
every 3,000 miles (well...you should); you need to do the same
with your body. Keep those doctor appointments for physicals,
eye exams, mammograms, colonoscopies. And in the meantime,
pay attention to what your body is trying to tell you.

When you do yoga, you learn to listen to the sound of
your own breath. Breathing in and out. It teaches you to pay
attention to your fingers as you spread them on the mat, to your
toes as you lift up on them, to your torso as you turn it into a
simple twist.

One of the best things about yoga, tai chi and other forms of meditative practices is that they increase your body awareness—and that alone can reduce your risk of depression and anxiety, decrease insomnia and stress-related inflammation, and boost immunity, according to numerous studies conducted by the National Institutes of Health.

Listen to your body, let it talk to you, and it will tell you what it needs—and what you need.

EXERCISE

Name Your Tells

Sit down comfortably, cross-legged, close your eyes and just listen. Listen to your body. What is it telling you? Where does it feel good? Where is it sore? Where does it ache? What do you think it's trying to tell you?

Your body will tell you when it's hungry or tired or frustrated. Listen and do something about it. It's taken me a long time to learn this—and I still need reminding from time to time. I tend to overextend myself and often struggle to do everything on my list for the day. I'll keep on going long past what is good for my body or my sanity. This is when I break something—the dinner plate that slips out of my hands as I carry it to the sink, the glass of milk I knock over on the kitchen table, the little toe I stub so hard I break it when I stumble into furniture. This is my body literally running me into things until I listen and stop and rest.

Your body has these tells, too. Make a list: Do your eyes start to twitch? Does the pain in your lower back worsen? Do you drop things? Trip over your own two feet? How does your body react to stress, to fatigue, to frustration? Learn to recognize these tells—and respond accordingly: sit down, take a break, take a nap, go to bed. For your own sake and for your body's sake, too.

Eat Well

"The food you eat can be either
the safest and most powerful form of medicine or the
slowest form of poison."
—Ann Wigmore

___

WE ALL KNOW WE'RE SUPPOSED to eat well and we all
know what that means. It means we're supposed to eat good
food, or as Michael Pollan likes to say (and I'm paraphrasing
here): Eat real food, that is, food that came from a plant—not
food that was made in a plant.

No processed food, no fast food, no crap food. Eat fruits and
vegetables, protein, complex carbs.

It's not rocket science: Just fill your fridge with fruits and
vegetables and lean protein. Or drive past that McDonald's to a
soup-and-salad place.

But we don't necessarily do that. And by not doing it, we
set ourselves up for early death. A poor diet is the second most
common predictor of early death after smoking. Eat a diet long
on salt and short on whole grains, fruit, nuts, seeds and fish oils,

and you'll die too young from a host of diseases, most notably heart disease, cancer and stroke, according to the massive, ongoing Global Burden of Disease study.

If you're thinking, well, we're living longer than ever, that's true—but more of our lives are spent in poor health. A nutritious diet can help us avoid that fate. The healthiest cuisines in the world—based on longevity—are the Mediterranean, New Nordic, Japanese and French diets, according to an exhaustive study of 187 countries funded by Bill and Melinda Gates and reported in the *Lancet Global Health* medical journal.

While as different as escargot and beets, herring and seaweed, Brussels sprouts and sushi, these diets do have commonalities: They all center on local and seasonal foods, notably vegetables and seafood. Processed food is limited, as is red meat.

Go ahead: Eat your veggies. You know you should.

EXERCISE

Keep a Food Diary

Keep a food diary. I know you've heard this before, but this is one that really, really works. Write down everything you eat for a week and you'll see when you are most likely to eat crap. Keeping a food diary has helped me see when I go astray: I eat crap when I do not take the time to prepare—or if I'm on the road, track down—nutritious meals. Or when I'm facing a long day and I keep grabbing whatever is at hand to keep going.

Keep a food diary and you'll learn what your trigger points are: when you get too tired, when your blood sugar is low, when you fail to eat properly or regularly, when you eat too little or too much.

Your body deserves good fuel. Yet many of us treat our bodies as if they were junkyard cars running on doughnut grease, instead of Cadillacs running on high-octane gasoline.

It's time to wise up—to treat your body well, feed it well. It's the only one you've got.

——·I HAPPY PILLS ·——

How Hangry Are You?

"A hungry stomach cannot hear."
—Jean de La Fontaine

Hangry—meaning so hungry you're angry and upset and irritable—has now been recognized as a word by the *Oxford English Dictionary.*

Hangry is not only a real word, it's a real thing. Scientists say being hangry is one of our human survival mechanisms, triggering us into action when our blood sugar levels dip too low and we need to eat. That still holds true: An Ohio State University study found couples argue more when their blood sugar levels are low—and some researchers believe there's a link between low glucose levels and violent behavior as well.

I know—from paying attention to my body—that both my energy level and my good mood suffer when I don't get enough protein. Or when I try to swap in sugars and simple carbs for protein. Why? Because protein is key to stabilizing blood sugar levels.

Hangry is me personified when I skip too many meals or eat crap. Or, as my father-in-law used to say: "She's a lovely girl until she gets hungry. Better feed her."

I'm just saying.

Get a Massage

"The way to health is to have an aromatic bath and a
scented massage every day."
—Hippocrates

THE ANCIENT GREEKS WERE RIGHT. Massage is good for
you, and the only thing better than getting a massage is getting
one on a regular basis. Massage therapy pays off in physical and
emotional well-being, lessening anxiety, fatigue, depression
and back pain, and relieving symptoms from asthma and HIV.
The positive benefits of massage remain in effect for up to a
week, and the more massage sessions, the more sustainable
these effects are over time, according to a study in the *Journal of
Alternative and Complementary Medicine.*

I'm always surprised by the number of people I meet
who've never had a massage. I resisted myself for years—
and then my neck and shoulders froze up after I wrote a
book in two weeks, spending 20 hours a day hunched over
my laptop. A friend treated me to a massage. It was nothing
short of a revelation.

I should have known—because I'd been giving massages for years. Starting when I was a kid and my dad was a middle-aged soldier in paratrooper school. Keeping up with the 18-year-olds—and the 200 push-ups a day—was killing him. My kneading his shoulders helped. I would rub my kids' heads and backs and shoulders, too. To this day, when my all-grown-up kids come home, they say, "Oh, Mom. Could you give me a massage?"

Getting a massage is self-care—and self-love—at its best. Indulge yourself.

EXERCISE
Get—and Give—a Massage

The best thing about yoga is that it's a form of self-massage. Your body loves it because you're twisting and turning and pressing—and in the process, the poses become a form of self-massage. Even better is the Thai massage we studied during our yoga teacher training. The best part: We students practiced 10 hours a day on each other. Even though giving massages for hours can be very strenuous—exhausting for your fingers and hands and arms, even back and neck and shoulders and legs if you're not careful—we always went home feeling great because for every massage we gave, we got one in return.

Find a buddy and give each other massages. Your respective bodies will thank you.

Moderation

———

"Be moderate in order to taste
the joys of life in abundance."
—Epicurus

———

IN A WORLD where the sands are always shifting beneath our feet, moderation is the sanest route to happiness. It's also the safest course, given the fact that we never really know how much of anything is good for us.

Take coffee.

Since I started drinking coffee back in the '80s, coffee has had more ups and downs than my own roller-coaster life: Coffee's good for you, coffee's bad for you. Drink as much coffee as you want, limit your coffee to two cups a day, tops. Drink decaffeinated coffee, drink half-caffeinated coffee, drink fully caffeinated coffee.

Same thing with alcohol and exercise and fat and red meat and dairy and practically every other thing you can name.

But you'll never go wrong if you do everything in moderation. A little goes a long way, and a little every day goes the furthest of all.

EXERCISE

A List of Excesses

If moderation is our friend, then excess is our enemy. As Hippocrates said, "Everything in excess is opposed by nature."

Make a list of your excesses. Be honest. Brutally honest.

And don't just list your vices. Remember, even your virtues can work against you when you overuse them. Take a hard look at what you pride yourself on.

Maybe you pride yourself on being a hard worker. But there's a fine line between working hard and workaholism.

Or maybe you like to think of yourself as a weekend warrior, making up for your lack of activity during the week with power workouts on the weekends. But you may be overdoing it and risking injury.

You get the idea.

Ask yourself these questions: What do you do too much of? What do you do too little of? How can you moderate the effects on your body?

Have a
Glass of Wine

"Wine is the most healthful and
most hygienic of beverages."
—Louis Pasteur

HAVE A GLASS OF WINE. Not beer. Not hard liquor. Drink
wine, and you'll enjoy a mortality rate 34 percent lower than
your beer- and spirits-chugging pals, according to a Finnish
study reported in the *Journals of Gerontology*.

Specifically, drink red wine. Red wine is a bountiful source
of resveratrol, a plant compound found in red wine, grapes,
berries and peanuts. Resveratrol acts like an antioxidant,
suggesting that moderate consumption may help boost
longevity, help prevent some cancers, lower blood pressure,
reduce the risk of heart disease, boost immunity and improve
mental health, according to numerous studies.

Not to mention unwind after a long day.

Note: These benefits are only associated with moderate drinking, defined as, "Up to one drink per day for women, and up to two drinks per day for men, and only by adults of legal drinking age," by the *Dietary Guidelines for Americans.*

EXERCISE

Trading Places

A glass of wine with dinner is a good thing, especially if you've got type 2 diabetes. According to a study reported in the *Annals of Internal Medicine*, drinking a glass of wine with dinner may help lower glucose levels—and improve glucose metabolism.

Again, drinking red wine with your supper provides more benefit than white wine, most notably a boost in HDL, the good cholesterol.

If you like a glass of wine in the evening, save it for dinner. Here are some pairings you might try:

- Pinot Noir and Anchovy Pizza
- Merlot and Cajun Blackened Salmon
- Riesling and Sweet & Sour Chicken
- Chardonnay and Dungeness Crab
- Sauvignon Blanc and Pasta Primavera
- Cabernet Sauvignon and Moussaka

Have Sex

"Good sex is like good bridge. If you don't have a good
partner, you'd better have a good hand."
—Mae West

HAVING SEX MAKES YOU HAPPY. As we've seen in Happier
Together, sex is critical to maintaining a happy relationship.
But the benefits of having sex go beyond helping couples be
happier together. In addition to all those lovely stress-relieving
hormones, numerous studies reveal that having regular sex:

- Helps manage pain
- Lowers cholesterol
- Deepens sleep
- Boosts immune system
- Improves bladder control
- Protects against heart disease and Alzheimer's
- Promotes longevity

And you don't need a partner to have sex. You can enjoy the
benefits of an orgasm all by yourself. Be the master of your own

destiny and make yourself feel good, with or without a partner.

EXERCISE

Once a Week

Are you having enough sex? Many of us are not. And it may surprise you to learn that the people having less sex—and the people having more sex—are not necessarily who you think they are.

Younger millennials—defined as those born in the 1990s—are having the least sex of any generation in 60 years, according to a study published in *Archives of Sexual Behavior*. Reasons range from workaholism and fear of commitment to body shaming and antidepressants (which can dampen sexual desire).

Back in the last decades of the 20th century, Americans had sex 60 to 65 times a year. That dropped to 53 times per year by 2014. Even married couples—who typically have more sex than single people—are only getting it on 56 times a year these days, compared to 67 times a year back in 1989. You can blame stress and prestige television and all the other forms of entertainment available to us (including porn).

The only people having more sex are septuagenarians, who are hooking up nearly once a month, up from only 9.6 times a year 30 years ago.

No matter what your age, aim for more sex. At least once a week is ideal (see page 122). So make a sex date with your lover—or yourself—every week. Come hell or HBO.

┌ HAPPY PILLS ┐

Z is for Zinc

Zinc plays an important role in our well-being (and we're not just talking cold remedies here). This essential trace element helps our immune and digestive systems function and facilitates the production, growth and repair of hormones. Its anti-inflammatory properties may help our bodies fight cancer and reverse heart disease.

Zinc can also improve our ability to concentrate, maintain a nutritious diet, regulate our moods, enhance our fertility and even improve our sex lives. Best of all, zinc may help us boost and maintain positive feelings, most notably happiness, according to a study reported in *MicroNourish*.

Note: Not getting enough zinc can lead to many health problems, leaky gut syndrome and chronic fatigue syndrome among them. Vegans and vegetarians especially run the risk of zinc deficiency.

Foods rich in zinc:

- Lamb
- Beef
- Yogurt
- Oysters
- Eggs
- Mushrooms
- Beans
- Pumpkin seeds
- Cocoa powder
- Cashews
- Poultry
- Whole Grains

———

"Imagination is the beginning of creation.
You imagine what you desire, you will what you
imagine and at last you create what you will."
—George Bernard Shaw

———

(6)
Happier Brain

"The human brain has 100 billion neurons, each neuron connected to 10,000 other neurons. Sitting on your shoulders is the most complicated object in the known universe."
—Michio Kaku

Your brain—that complicated object—is where the control center of your happiness lives. It's a control center that, like the rest of your body, is driven by chemicals.

Happiness is good chemistry—a formula made up of neurochemicals. Get the formula right, and you feel a rainbow of positive emotions: joy, gratitude, hope, serenity, cheerfulness, contentment, admiration, love. Get the formula wrong, and happiness falters.

If this sounds like an oversimplification, well, it is. And it isn't. While there are myriad factors that determine our happiness— both external and internal—the truth remains that being happy when your brain chemistry is working against you is an uphill struggle. Today, 1 in 9 Americans take antidepressants—up from less than 1 in 50 Americans 30 years ago.

The good news is there's a lot you can do to entertain and engage your brain. To maintain that sweet balance of neurochemicals in that complicated object between your ears. To figure out the perfect formula for your particular brain chemistry. In Happier Brain, we'll take a look at what you can do to keep that big human brain of yours—a brain wider than the sky, to quote Emily Dickinson—healthy and happy.

Just as a healthy body is a happy body, a healthy brain is a happy brain.

And a happy brain is a happy you—neurochemicals and all.

Learn Something New

"Live as if you were to die tomorrow.
Learn as if you were to live forever."
—Mahatma Gandhi

THE BRAIN IS A LEARNING MACHINE. Learning is what it's programmed to do—and from the moment we're born, our brains help us learn what we need to know to navigate our lives—from reading, writing and arithmetic to composing a symphony or creating a new computer language.

A bored brain is an unhappy brain. Challenge your brain and you'll challenge yourself to be both smarter and happier. This holds true no matter your age. A study reported in *Psychological Science* revealed that older people who learn a new skill—such as quilting or digital photography—experience a significant and sustained boost in memory that could postpone cognitive aging.

Learning something new takes time and patience. It takes

practice—and that practice rewires your brain, strengthening the vital connections between your neurons. As a result, your neurons fire more efficiently. And more happily.

Keep your neurons happy. Learn something new.

EXERCISE

Novelty 101

When's the last time you tackled something completely new? Something that took you out of your current comfort zone—whether it was as exotic as learning ancient Greek or prosaic as doing your own taxes?

I confess to being one of those dorks with a low boredom threshold who loves learning new things. Being a writer makes this easy: Every project takes me deep into subjects I know nothing about—from 18th century American art to today's military working dogs. Being a writer also means I sit on my butt thinking, so I need more physically demanding experiences as well. To that end, I took up ballroom dancing at 36, horseback riding at 42, boxing at 49 and yoga at 53.

Find something new you've always wanted to learn: fencing or Russian or high stakes poker. Sign up for a class or private lessons. The sooner the better. Think of it as a gift that keeps on giving...for your brain.

Travel to a
New Place

―――

"But that's the glory of foreign travel, as far as I am concerned. I don't want to know what people are talking about. I can't think of anything that excites a greater sense of childlike wonder than to be in a country where you are ignorant of almost everything. Suddenly you are 5 years old again. You can't read anything, you have only the most rudimentary sense of how things work, you can't even reliably cross a street without endangering your life. Your whole existence becomes a series of interesting guesses."
—Bill Bryson

―――

THE CALL OF THE OPEN ROAD. There's nothing like it— especially for your brain. Your brain loves a challenge— and nothing is more challenging than a new environment. So much novelty for your novelty-loving brain to process: new places, new people, new languages, new navigation, new stimuli everywhere.

I confess that for me, travel is an addiction. I love being home in the New England countryside—2 miles from the nearest gas station and gallon of milk—but luckily the travel I do for business and pleasure gives the nomad in me just enough attention to keep cabin fever at bay. I'm on the road about one week per month, and this country-mouse/city-mouse schedule is perfect for me. And for my overall health and well-being.

A number of studies show that people who travel regularly are happier, healthier, more fit, less-stressed and may even live longer than those who do not. Plus, travel helps you build strong antibodies, boosting your immunity; improve your mood, decreasing depression; and lower your risk of heart disease.

The effects on your brain are dramatic, according to the *Journal of Personality and Social Psychology*, and you'll enhance your cognitive flexibility and your creativity. Go abroad, and you'll be more open-minded and emotionally stable.

Time to hit the road.

EXERCISE

Throw That Dart

Visit somewhere you've never been before—somewhere that takes you out of your comfort zone. That's where your brain will have to play the hardest to keep up.

When my daughter moved to Europe, I was not that excited about traveling there, apart from the joy of seeing her. As an Army brat, I'd spent half of my childhood in Germany and seen much of Europe in the process. Been there, done that, I thought.

But I couldn't have been more wrong. Now I travel abroad at least once a year to see my international family, which includes Swiss-American and British-American grandchildren. Together we've gone to Paris, Madrid, Dublin, London, Lausanne, Corfu, the south of France and northern Italy, among other places. Sometimes it's a place I choose, and other times it's a place I'd never choose—and regardless it's fun, stimulating and exhausting all at once.

The next time you plan a trip—at least once a year for the sake of your brain—choose somewhere unlikely. Throw a dart at a map and go where it takes you.

Embrace the Arts

"Art is everywhere, except it has to
pass through a creative mind."
—Louise Nevelson

THERE IS NOTHING LIKE art to stimulate our brains. The
National Institute of Mental Health (NIMH) research reveals
that just looking at art activates those parts of the brain that
process emotion and engages the brain's pleasure and reward
systems. What's more: Visit an art gallery or museum and you'll
lower your stress level and your cortisol levels, according to a
University of Westminster study.

I love museums so much that when we travel, my family
sets limits on how many museums we'll visit, just to keep my
addiction in check. That said, when I'm alone, I can do what I
want. And if I cry (I cry a lot in museums), I don't embarrass the
children. Whenever I'm in Manhattan—around a dozen times a
year—I go to The Met or the Museum of Modern Art just for the
glory of all that beauty, which inevitably reduces me to tears. It's
a good cry.

When was the last time you indulged your inner art lover? Give your brain a break—and a treat!—and go see a Picasso.

EXERCISE

Make Art

The only thing better for your brain than seeing art is making art. Producing art not only enhances your motor skills, it also enhances cognitive processes, particularly in areas such as introspection, self-monitoring and memory, according to a study reported in *PLOS ONE Journal*. The overall result: significant boosts in emotional resiliency as well as brain activity.

Given these benefits, art therapy is now being used to help treat Alzheimer's patients. Making art can help patients recall lost memories and help them communicate better, according to research reported in the *Canadian Journal of Neurological Sciences*.

Make some art of your own. Paint a picture, make a collage, draw a portrait. If it's been so long you don't know where to start, borrow a kid, a box of crayons and some construction paper. Plan a project together—a birthday card for mom, a picture for granddad, a holiday decoration—and go for it.

Keep Moving

"It is exercise alone that supports
the spirits and keeps the mind in vigor."
—Marcus Tullius Cicero

THE BEST WAY to keep your brain happy and healthy is to get moving. Exercise benefits your body and your brain—right down to the molecular level. In fact, a University of Georgia study revealed that just 20 minutes of exercise helps your brain process information more easily and enhances memory.

Increase your heart rate on a regular basis and you'll increase the size of your hippocampus, the part of your brain devoted to long term memory, according to a University of British Columbia study. People who exercise have bigger prefrontal cortexes and medial temporal cortexes than people who don't. These are the areas of your brain that control thinking and memory.

You read that right: Work out and you'll have a bigger brain. Literally. And when it comes to brains, bigger really is better.

I know, I know, like you needed another reason to start an

exercise program. As if getting stronger and fitter and healthier weren't enough. Now you can be smarter too.

All you have to do is break a sweat.

EXERCISE

The Big Brain Workout

If I told you I credit exercise with helping me achieve my most meaningful life goals, you might think "whatever." But looking back at my greatest career successes, I can see that they coincide with the periods in which I did the most consistent and vigorous exercise.

Take a look at your life and see if the same holds true. Granted, this is anecdotal, but given what we know about the brain, it wouldn't be such a surprise, would it?

Countless writers—Rumi, Nietzsche, Dickens, Thoreau, Hemingway, Thomas Jefferson, Mark Twain and Jim Butcher among them—believed long walks were critical to their creative process. Haruki Murakami runs, J.M. Coetzee cycles, Barack Obama shoots hoops, Anna Wintour plays tennis, Arianna Huffington does yoga, Nick Woodman surfs, and on and on.

Follow the example of these successful people: Set a career goal and an exercise goal at the same time. The one with the most goals wins.

Practice Mindfulness

"Be where you are;
otherwise you will miss your life."
—Buddha

MINDFULNESS IS simply paying attention to your life as you live it. Learn to do this, and your brain will be much happier—not to mention your life.

If this sounds woo-woo to you, consider the studies conducted by Harvard Medical School and Massachusetts General Hospital (among others) and reported in the *Harvard Business Review*. This research reveals that people doing a mindfulness practice like meditation enjoy serious enlargements in the density of their brains' gray matter. Mindfulness also:

- Improves self-regulation
- Optimizes decision-making
- Boosts pain tolerance
- Stabilizes emotions
- Alleviates anxiety

- Enhances memory
- Increases resilience
- Sharpens complex thinking skills
- Improves perception
- Strengthens sense of self
- Protects against toxic stress

And that's just what a little mindfulness can do for your brain.

Take a seat, inhale, exhale, clear your mind. Or roll out your mat and do a little yoga. Or take a stroll and do a walking meditation.

Om your way to a happier brain.

EXERCISE

Pay Attention Now

Stop what you're doing. Right now. Put this book down, close your eyes and focus on your breath for a full minute, breathing in and out. Go ahead. I'll wait.

Breathe in, breathe out. Breathe like a baby. That is, don't pull your stomach in when you inhale. Instead, expand your belly. Hold it at the top of your breath for a count of three, then slowly exhale. Inhale, inflate a balloon. Exhale, let the air out of the balloon.

It's that simple.

Whenever you find yourself stressing out, focus on your breath. When you learn to mind your breath, you'll know what it means to be mindful.

Keep practicing. But first, finish reading this book.

Let It Go

"In the end, just three things matter:
How well we have lived
How well we have loved
How well we have learned to let go."
—Jack Kornfield

WHEN A FRIEND OF MINE was going through a bad time,
I bought her a poster that featured a yogi meditating in the
lotus position. These words ran across the top of the print:
Let that s--t go.

My friend was blaming herself for the actions of others,
feeling guilty and anxious and depressed over the deterioration
of those relationships with them. We've all had this happen—
friendships, work relationships, romantic attachments, familial
ties that die slowly or blaze out quickly due to disagreements or
disappointments or just plain neglect.

The best thing to do—and, admittedly, the hardest thing—
is to let those disagreements and disappointments and
relationship deaths go. The sooner you do, the better you'll feel—

and the faster you'll let go of your past and get on with your present.

Hint: There's a reason it's called "present."

EXERCISE

Let Go—Or Be Dragged

That's what the magnet on my refrigerator says. It's a reminder to me that whenever I hold on to something too hard, I live to regret it.

Make a list of the things you've held onto for too long. How did you get dragged? What are you holding on to now that you should let go of? How might you do that before you get dragged? Make a plan.

Rest Your Brain

———

"Idleness is not just a vacation,
an indulgence or a vice; it is as indispensable to the
brain as vitamin D is to the body,
and deprived of it we suffer a mental affliction as
disfiguring as rickets."
—Tim Kreider

———

WAKING REST—AS OPPOSED TO SLEEPING— is as
important to a happy and healthy brain as sleep itself.
The brain performs similar molecular, genetic and physiological
processes critical to our cognitive well-being while we're asleep
and at rest.

According to numerous studies reported in *Scientific
American*, our brains work hard during the day—and a little
downtime gives our brains the break needed to get back on
track, helping us to pay attention, boost our motivation and
productivity, enhance creativity, even build our memories and
reinforce our ethics. In short, waking rest not only helps us
perform our best, it helps us be our best self.

If you're thinking, yeah, just let me tell my boss that when she catches me daydreaming—well, you should. Some of the most successful, hard-driving Fortune 500 companies—Google, Apple, Facebook, Coca-Cola, Green Mountain Coffee and Ford among them—now encourage workers to take multiple short breaks during the workday. It's a strategy that pays off, especially in terms of employee engagement.

EXERCISE

Daydreaming for Fun and Profit

If daydreaming is, as Deepak Chopra puts it, "the source of infinite creativity," then we should all spend more time daydreaming. Science backs this up; people who daydream on a regular basis tend to be more creative and intelligent than people who don't, according to a Georgia Institute of Technology study.

Like most writers, I spend a lot of time daydreaming, which I like to call work. You're laughing, but I'm not alone. Look at George Lucas, who famously said that, like many of us, he spent most of his time in school daydreaming and "managed to turn it into a living."

Give yourself permission to daydream on a daily basis. Indulge your brain. Let your mind wander wherever it will. Don't be surprised if you daydream your way to a new breakthrough, a new discovery, a new you.

---| HAPPY PILLS |---

The Happiest Man in the World

A Tibetan monk and geneticist named Matthieu Ricard has been named the happiest man in the world—thanks to his brain, which produces the highest levels of gamma waves neuroscientists have ever seen. Off the charts high, according to the University of Wisconsin study.

Gamma waves are brain waves linked to peak performance, focus and memory. As your level of gamma wave activity goes up, so does your mood, your capacity for empathy and your ability to feel compassion. In other words: bliss.

Ricard not only has crazy-high gamma waves, he also has a left prefrontal cortex that's far busier than its right counterpart, confirming an extraordinary predisposition for happiness and a disinclination for negativity.

Ricard attributes his happiness to meditation. Not surprising since he's a Tibetan monk. But the neuroscientists also studied the brains of other monks as well, finding similar patterns. These changes in cognitive function were most profound in those who'd been meditating for years, but even those who had been meditating for less than a month showed some change.

Meditation: Not just for monks any more.

Disconnect

> "We all need the pendulum swing of snatching spaces of
> solitude and serving tables of sociability.
> In fact, the more plugged in and connected we are,
> the more we need to unplug and disconnect.
> A world of presence needs a time of absence."
> **—Leonard Sweet**

SAY UNPLUG in the 21st century and the assumption is that
you mean disconnecting from electronics. But even though it
may feel like the source of all modern stress is related to the
devices that increasingly run our lives, there are lots more
stress-inducing factors that can impact your physical, emotional
and mental health. Among some of the top stressors:

- Death of a loved one
- Losing your job
- Moving
- Having a difficult conversation
- Being the victim of a crime
- Illness/injury

- Divorce
- Having a baby
- Financial trouble
- Legal trouble

Change of any kind brings with it an enormous amount of stress. Too much stress can sensitize you to stress going forward, making it even harder on your brain. This is why you need to disconnect, not just from your smartphone, but from your whole life from time to time.

EXERCISE

Sign up to Disconnect

Taking time out to disconnect can be stressful in and of itself. So take the stress out of it. Sign up for a class or a club or an appointment to do something that takes you—and your brain—out of your "real life." In other words, do something that requires a little make-believe:

- Take an acting class
- Join the Society for Creative Anachronism
- Play *Dungeons & Dragons*
- Spend the day getting a makeover
- Go to a Renaissance fair
- Go to a costume party

Or play dress-up with your children, or the children of your friends. Host a tea party, brandish a lightsaber, build a Lego city. They'll love it—and so will you.

Go Outside

"I've never had a really creative idea sitting
at my desk. All the big ideas that made a difference
happened when I was playing outside."
—Barbara Corcoran

WHEN I WAS A KID, parents sent us "out to play" and we
didn't come back until dinner time or dark—whichever came
first. Those days are gone, which is really too bad. Nearly half
of preschool kids do not play outside today—and most of the
little time they do play outside amounts to recess at school or
scheduled play breaks at daycare.

Playing outside is good for kids—improving vision,
increasing attention span, lowering stress levels, building social
skills and boosting all-important vitamin D levels, according
to multiple studies. Notably, research from the University
of Missouri-Kansas City revealed playing outside is good for
children's growing brains, fostering "social, emotional and
cognitive competencies."

What's good for kids is good for grown-ups, too. A University of East Anglia international study revealed spending time outdoors offers many health benefits, from lowering the risk of type 2 diabetes, heart disease, premature death and preterm birth to even boosting immunity. Time outdoors will even help you get a good night's sleep. The best part: Going outside lowers the stress hormones, most notably cortisol, that we've seen can adversely affect brain function.

Your mother was right (again): Go out and play. It's good for your brain.

EXERCISE

Walkabout Your Brain

One of the best things you can do for your mental health is borrow from the Japanese concept of forest bathing and take a walk in a green space (if not an actual forest). Turns out it's as good for your brain as it is for your body. According to a Stanford University study, people who walk in green spaces experience a calm born of the changes that take place in the brain. Walk down a tree-lined path and you'll experience a boost in mental health—improving your mood and quieting the subgenual prefrontal cortex, the part of your brain responsible for brooding. Brooding is a precursor to depression, and there's nothing happy about that.

When I was a kid, my dad used to take me for long walks with the dogs through the woods. It was my special time with him, with the dogs, with nature—and I loved it. I loved the clean scent pines, the musky odor of the earth, the squirrels skittering in the trees. Now we live on 19 acres of sugar maples, woods all around. Lovely in every season: the signature green of spring, the thick canopy of summer, the colorful leaves of autumn, the bare trunks of winter. The dogs love it—and so do I. On our walks, I brood about my novel in progress, and that brooding inevitably takes a turn for the better, right into brainstorming.

Take your brain for a walk in the woods. (Remember: If you live in the city, you're at a greater risk for depression and anxiety than your peers who live in greener places. Consider that an incentive.)

You don't have to go very far. Find somewhere that's green and go there. Even in the chaos of New York City there's Central Park. Go green and get happy.

Indulge
Your Curiosity

"Never lose a holy curiosity."
—Albert Einstein

NOTHING LEADS US to more engaging experiences than
our own curiosity. Curiosity is nature's way of honing our
survival skills, prompting us to seek out new people, new places,
new things—and in the process, rewarding our exploration
by releasing feel-good chemicals in the brain. Plus, when we
indulge our curiosity, we feel more positive, less anxious and
more content with ourselves and our lives, according to a study
published by the *Journal of Personality*.

Children explore the world around them quite naturally—
think of the last time you took a child to the beach for the first
time or presented her with a new toy—but sometimes we grown-
ups forget how.

While a new experience can be stressful—be it a trip abroad
or a ride on a zip line—meeting the challenge only intensifies

the pleasure we experience when we do it. The trick is to build opportunities for exploration right into our daily lives. Curiosity leads to engagement, and engagement leads to happiness.

EXERCISE

Name Your Curiosities

Make a list of people you'd love to meet, places you'd love to see and things you'd love to do. Think outside the box and your comfort zone; don't stop until you have 52 experiences. Include simple, inexpensive entries—try that new coffee shop, invite that colleague three cubicles down to lunch, trade in your sneakers for snow shoes this winter—as well as more complex experiences like learning Japanese, hosting an elaborate dinner party or starting your own podcast. Throw in some over-the-top and (perhaps) once-in-a-lifetime opportunities—writing a book, volunteering abroad, climbing Mount Kilimanjaro—as well.

Write each one on a slip of paper and put it in a jar. Each week for the next year, retrieve one—and do it. You can at least get a running start: Write that first page, sign up for that class, research that trip. Indulge your curiosity and have some fun doing it. You'll be all the happier for it.

Feed Your Brain

"What you eat directly affects the structure and function of your brain and, ultimately, your mood."
—Eva Selhub

YOUR BRAIN IS A GREEDY BEAST that uses up 20 percent of the calories you consume. Every time your heart beats, your arteries deliver 15 to 20 percent of your blood to your little gray cells, using 20 percent of the oxygen and fuel carried along by that blood. And that's on a normal day. Think hard, and your brain may gobble up even more of that fuel and oxygen.

This is why eating well is as important to your brain as it is to the rest of your body. Without sufficient nutrition, your brain will suffer—and so will you. Here's a list of the most important brain foods that you should eat on a regular basis, according to the Rush University Medical Center:

- Green leafy vegetables
- More vegetables
- Nuts

- Berries
- Beans
- Whole grains
- Fish
- Poultry
- Olive oil
- Wine (in moderation)

You should also limit your intake of red meat, butter and margarine, cheese, pastries and sweets, fried foods and fast foods. But you already knew that.

EXERCISE

Protein for Breakfast

You know you're supposed to eat breakfast, but what you eat is as important as when you eat it. Neurotransmitters—the messengers that carry signals from one brain cell to another—are made up of the amino acids that make up protein. The faster and more efficiently these messengers carry those signals, the better our brain cells work. Asking your brain to work well after hours without fuel—why do you think they call it "break fast?"—is unrealistic. And the fact that these neurotransmitters are made up of protein, well, that's why you need a good protein-based meal in the morning.

Protein doesn't just make us smarter, it makes us happier too. Protein boosts our serotonin and dopamine levels, those feel-good neurotransmitters that reduce anxiety, boost energy, manage pain, improve sleep, clear our minds and just plain help us feel happy.

So, make sure you get enough protein—starting with breakfast. Skip the doughnuts and go for lean protein and complex carbs: a smoothie with milk or yogurt, an egg and cheese on a multigrain roll, peanut butter on multigrain toast, a protein shake, oatmeal and milk.

Try this for a week and see the difference. You may even drop a pound or two. According to a Tel Aviv University study, protein-rich breakfasts help you lose weight—especially when you eat whey protein, which tamps down ghrelin, the hangry hormone. Good sources of whey protein: ricotta cheese, milk, yogurt. You'll also find it in whey-based protein powders.

Don't forget your kids: They perform better at school when they have protein-rich meals in the morning.

Empty Your Mind

"A full mind is an empty bat."
—Branch Rickey

I LOVE BASEBALL. Baseball has the best quotes and the best stories and the best movies of all sports. If you're thinking that baseball has nothing to do with enlightenment, well, I beg to differ. I could make that case, but that's another book.

Back to Branch Rickey, the Hall of Fame player and manager best known for breaking the color barrier when he signed baseball great Jackie Robinson. A man ahead of his time, Rickey created the farm system and introduced the spring training complex, the batting tee, batting helmet and batting cage, among other innovations.

Rickey understood the importance of an empty mind. This is the opposite of what in meditation we call "monkey mind," the stress-driven thoughts of worry and regret and frustration that bounce off the walls of our chaotic minds too much of the time. Meditation is one way to quiet the monkey mind, as is yoga or tai chi or running.

But there are other ways to empty your mind as well. Any repetitive task we do often enough to do "without thinking" can help us empty our minds: washing the dishes, knitting, snapping beans, kneading dough, waxing the car, weeding the garden, etc.

As the Zen Buddhists say: "Before enlightenment: Chop wood, carry water. After enlightenment: Chop wood, carry water."

Or just swing that bat.

EXERCISE

Getting Thee to a Batting Cage

When you were a kid, what did you like to do so much that you did it over and over again? Skip stones, hit tennis balls, jump rope, color, weave those little potholders?

When I was a kid, I played endless games of fetch with my little poodle, Rogue. I tossed, he retrieved. Over and over and over again.

My daughter took long nature walks everyday with her little Corgi, collecting sticks and shells and stones and whatever else struck her fancy.

My elder son—the kid they told me had a short attention span—spent hours shooting hoops after school—and wouldn't come in until it was too dark to see the basket.

My younger son loved blocks as a baby, devoting much time and attention to setting them up and knocking them down, countless times a day. As he grew older, he moved on from blocks to Lego to playing cards.

Whatever helped you empty your mind as a child will help you empty your mind now. Find a grown-up version of this same activity. Take it up once more.

Do Nothing

"*Il bel far niente* means 'the beauty of doing nothing'...
[it] has always been a cherished Italian ideal.
The beauty of doing nothing is the goal of all your work,
the final accomplishment for which you are
most highly congratulated. The more exquisitely
and delightfully you can do nothing,
the higher your life's achievement. You don't necessarily
need to be rich in order to experience this, either."
—Elizabeth Gilbert

LEAVE IT TO THE ITALIANS to raise doing nothing to a high art. To our busy-is-best American sensibility, this may seem like an exotic, if not downright suspect, idea. Blame our Puritan work ethic or our 24/7 culture or our tech-fueled futurism, but whatever—it's time to get over it.

Time to learn to do nothing with the same passion and perfection as the Italians.

When my daughter got married in Switzerland, my boys and I flew there for the wedding. The reception was held in a chalet in the Alps, a beautiful setting, for Switzerland is nothing if not beautiful. But my boys were not impressed. They were hangry.

After a week of what they considered way too much hiking and way too few calories, we took the train from Switzerland to Italy. Our plan was to spend the night before flying home the next day.

We had 24 hours in which to do nothing, a welcome thought after a week's stay in a very rigorously regimented and regulated state. We stayed in a small unremarkable village with one small unremarkable hotel and one small unremarkable restaurant, both situated on the small, unremarkable town square. Eventually we went out to eat at the restaurant, ordering antipasto and pizza and wine and coffee and melted chocolate bombe cake. Because this was Italy, it was a remarkable experience. The food, the ambiance, the service—the everything. It was hands-down perfection.

"Let's come back to this country," said my 12-year-old son.

His big brother agreed.

Don't get me wrong: Switzerland is a grand country—but they don't know *il bel far niente*.

EXERCISE

---

24 Hours of Nothing

Get in touch with your inner Italian. Spend an entire day doing absolutely nothing. If this kind of joyful indolence is truly beyond you, pack yourself off to a spa or the beach for the day—or better yet, go to Italy and experience *la dolce vita* firsthand.

Last year, my younger son—25 by this time—and I finally went back to Europe together. My daughter was pregnant with grandchild No. 3 and under doctor's orders not to spend more than five hours in a car at a time. Which meant that if we were to visit another country—which we couldn't wait to do—we needed to stay within a five-hour radius of the Alps. To my son, that meant only one thing: northern Italy. We piled into the car and headed for the Piedmont region. We toured the Royal Palace of Turin, the Egyptian Museum and Sacra di San Michele. Then we went to a convent-turned-hotel in the country and did what Italians do: nothing but eat pasta and drink Barolo wine and swim in the pool. Or, to show off the two words I learned there: *meriggiare*, meaning "to escape the heat of the midday sun by resting in the shade," and *abbiocco*, meaning "the drowsiness that follows eating a big meal."

We're still talking about it.

Book that trip to Italy—or anywhere else you can find some peace and quiet—and learn to do nothing, once and for all.

——————————— **HAPPY PILLS** ———————————

Vitamin F

Vitamin F is vital to our sense of well-being. The physical benefits of this collection of essential fatty acids—namely omega-3 fatty acids and omega-6 fatty acids—are well-known, ranging from reducing the risk of coronary thrombosis and stroke, lowering blood pressure, slowing hardening of the arteries, and easing symptoms of rheumatoid arthritis and poor circulation.

Yet just as important are the emotional benefits of vitamin F. According to the University of Maryland Medical Center, these fatty acids can help improve our memory, brain performance and behavioral function. Without them, we may find ourselves weary, depressed, moody or forgetful. In other words, not happy. Not happy at all.

(7)

Happier Heart

"Wherever you go, go with all your heart."
—Confucius

Win your heart. Lose your heart. Break your heart. Soft-hearted. Hard-hearted. Heart of gold. Heart of stone. Heart pounding, leaping, melting, sinking and (my personal favorite) bursting with joy.

The heart is the organ that pumps life-giving blood full of oxygen to all the cells of your body—but in our psyche and physiology, it's so much more. The heart is the center of life and love and emotion and happiness.

When I was doing my yoga teacher training, my back, shoulders and neck were too tight for me to do many of the poses involving those muscles at full expression—the result of a childhood injury and years of hunching over a computer. Michelle, my yoga teacher trainer, would just look at me when I walked into the studio and open her arms wide at her sides, bent at the elbow like goalposts. A sign to me to stretch those muscles across my chest and shoulders, giving me more range of motion. Try it now and you'll see how it opens your chest— and exposes your heart. In yoga, this is called opening the heart chakra—the energy center focused on love, compassion, kindness, harmony, self-acceptance, emotional integrity and forgiveness.

Opening your heart—that is, walking through the world with an open-hearted, relaxed-shoulder, aligned-spine posture—is as good for you physically as it is for you emotionally. In a study reported in the *Journal of the American Geriatrics Society*, posture is a reliable predictor of heart disease. People whose posture is bad— collapsed spine, compressed chest—are 2.4 times more likely to die of atherosclerosis.

In Happier Heart, we'll explore the many ways you can open your heart—and live a happier and healthier and longer life.

Work Up a Sweat

"Exercise should be regarded as tribute to the heart."
—Gene Tunney

EVERYONE KNOWS THAT exercise is good for our hearts. Study after study shows people who break a sweat on a regular basis are less likely to suffer or die from heart disease. New research conducted at the University of Maryland even reveals that just one 30-minute workout can change our hearts at the cellular level and keep us (literally) young at heart.

Work out regularly, and you'll improve your blood pressure, pulse rate and cholesterol levels—all critical to a healthy heart.

Get a good sweat going. According to the Harvard School of Public Health, the most effective heart-healthy exercises include walking, running and weight training. Mix it up for best results. And if none of these appeal to you, try activities such as rowing, biking, swimming, tennis or racquetball.

EXERCISE

Open Your Heart Exercise

Choose one of the heart-healthy exercises listed and do it for 30 minutes. If you're working out inside, enhance the experience with aromatherapy. Fill your diffuser or light some incense, using one of the following scents, all believed to help open your heart chakra: angelica, jasmine, marjoram, lavender, chamomile, rose, hyssop, melissa, geranium, ylang ylang, eucalyptus, peppermint, neroli, palmarosa, galbanum.

Set the mood with music designed for similar effect. Here's a sample playlist to get you going:

"Amazing Grace" by Renée Fleming

"Ganga Ma (Everlasting Love)" by Wah!

"I Won't Give Up" by Jason Mraz

"A Kiss To Build A Dream On" by Louis Armstrong

"L-O-V-E" by Nat King Cole

"A Love That Will Last" by Renee Olstead

"Mercy Now" by Mary Gauthier

"This Old Heart Of Mine" by Rod Stewart

"I Will Remember You" by Sarah McLachlan

"Vision Of Love" by Mariah Carey

"I Will Always Love You" by Whitney Houston

"Haven't Met You Yet" by Michael Bublé

"Sarab Nirantar" by Hari Bhajan

Do Random Acts of Kindness

"Carry out a random act of kindness,
with no expectation of reward, safe in the knowledge
that one day someone might do the same for you."
—Princess Diana

KINDNESS IS CONTAGIOUS. Do a kindness for someone, and it makes that someone feel good. (At least it should. If it doesn't make you feel good, see the next entry, "Receive Acts of Kindness.")

More importantly, being kind makes *you* feel good too. This is known as the "helper's high."

Most interesting of all, it makes whoever witnesses your kindness feel good as well. That's why a single act of kindness has a ripple effect. The more compassionate the act, the more good it does you, and the more good it does your heart—and the more good it does for those around you.

We see this phenomenon on social media all the time. For

example: A journalist posts a video of dogs being rescued from a locked cage as the floodwaters of Hurricane Florence rose around them. Lots of people share that post on social media, and the next thing you know you're messaging the journalist—along with thousands of other people—saying you'll be happy to give one or more of those dogs a forever home. And then you remember you never asked your family if it's OK before you volunteered—but they're fine with it. (Hey—don't pretend you don't do this too.)

Because kindness really is contagious.

EXERCISE

For Whom Kindness Tolls

The other day I was driving south on the Everett Turnpike from New Hampshire to Massachusetts on a toll road. Having once again forgotten to file for an E-ZPass, I pulled over to the toll booth to pay the $1 fare. The toll taker smiled and waved me on through the gate.

"The guy in that white truck in front of you paid your toll," the toll taker told me.

I'd heard of such gestures, of course, but this was the first time I'd knowingly been on the receiving end of a completely random act of kindness. Or the giving end, for that matter. While I pride myself on being kind to others and appreciating the kindnesses done to me, this mostly involves people I know or have met or have at least seen, if only on the meaner streets of Manhattan. Or charities with whom I have an affiliation, however tenuous: veteran groups, animal rescue organizations, children's funds, etc.

I've never paid someone else's toll. Frankly, it had never occurred to me to do so.

This truly random act of kindness made an impression on me. I vowed that the next time I went through a toll booth, I was going to pay the toll for the person behind me. Of course, I totally forgot. So now I have two bucks stuck in the visor on the driver's side of the car to remind me to do just that. Let's hope I remember.

Being kind is hard enough. Being kind at random is, as it turns out, even harder.

Let's keep on trying.

Receive Acts
of Kindness

"A little 'thank you' that you will say to someone
for a 'little favor' shown to you is a key to unlock
the doors that hide unseen 'greater favors.'
Learn to say 'thank you' and why not?"
—Israelmore Ayivor

WHEN I WAS GOING through my first divorce, I was young
and broke and under-employed with two young children to
support. My parents helped me in every way—providing moral
and financial support—so much so that, looking back, I have
no idea how I would have gotten through that terrible period
without them.

At the time, however, I was less than gracious. The deeper
my predicament and the harder I worked to get out of it, the
more I bristled whenever my parents helped me out. I needed
the assistance, not just for me but for my kids, but I hated

205

needing it. Finally, my father took me aside and told me I was being selfish.

That brought me up short. In our family, the worst possible thing anyone can call you is selfish or lazy. I knew I wasn't lazy—in fact I was working round the clock to pull us out of poverty—but I didn't see how he could call me selfish either. I said as much.

"You're always helping people," my dad told me. "Helping people makes you feel good. Yet you are denying us the pleasure of helping you. That's selfish. Just say thank you—and let us feel good too."

He was right. It was greedy of me to keep that helper's high all to myself. Ever since, I've tried to be more gracious about receiving kindnesses from others. Starting with my parents.

The next time someone helps you, just say thank you. And mean it.

EXERCISE

Write a Thank-You Note

Think of the people who have done the loveliest acts of kindness for you—large and small. Make a list of these fine men and women. Ask yourself if you've ever formally thanked them for their generosity.

Choose one of these benefactors and write a thank-you note. Express your sincere gratitude and appreciation. It doesn't matter if it's been years since the favor was granted—write it anyway. If you don't know where the person is, track him or her down. It's much easier these days.

Send that letter. It's always gratifying to receive a letter acknowledging a kindness—and even more gratifying to send one.

Note: Even if you learn that the person has since passed on, see that the next of kin receives the letter. Your benefactor's family will appreciate the gesture.

Cuddle with a Child

"I have learned that there is more power in a good strong hug than in a thousand meaningful words."
—Ann Hood

SCIENCE CONFIRMS WHAT common sense and good mothers have always known: The more affectionate the parents, the happier and more successful the child. According to studies reported in *Child Trends,* children blessed with warm and caring parents enjoy higher self-esteem, do better in school and suffer fewer psychological and behavioral issues than less fortunate kids. These benefits last until adulthood and beyond; kids who grow up with affectionate parents become happier and more resilient adults.

Showing physical affection to the children in our lives is important. Doing so will benefit us as well as them. Hugs, massages and cuddling all produce oxytocin, reducing stress, lowering blood pressure and heart rates and helping us feel happier.

Without such physical affection, we suffer what is known

as skin hunger, that is, a longing for skin-to-skin contact. Affection-deprived people suffer more anxiety and mood disorders, are more commitment-phobic, have less satisfying relationships and are more prone to immune disorders. Suffer from skin hunger and you're more apt to be lonely, depressed, stressed and generally less happy and less healthy, according to a study in *Psychology Today.*

Find a kid—one of your own or a close friend's—and cuddle. You'll both feel better.

EXERCISE

The Teddy Bear Solution

Skin hunger is such a powerful drive—right up there with the desire for food, drink, sex and shelter—that people who go too long without it may consider turning to other means of getting it if they have no close friends or family. Professional cuddlers—who'll give you a hug or hold you in a nonsexual, therapeutic way—are setting up shop in what *The New York Times* called "the latest thing in wellness."

But if you don't want to go that route, you may not have to look much further than your teddy bear. Just as children find comfort hugging their stuffed animals, we adults can find comfort, too, with touch therapy, in the form of inanimate objects that simulate human touch. Not only can cuddling with a teddy bear help relieve anxiety and depression, it can help people with low self-esteem feel better about themselves and their place in the world, according to a series of studies that appeared in *Psychological Science.* In short: Teddy bears are a hedge against existential angst.

Give a friend—or yourself—a teddy bear.

Make Good Friends

"A friend is what the heart needs all the time."
—Henry Van Dyke

WE ALL LOVE OUR BFFS—and with good reason. As it turns out, our circle of friends can influence our health and happiness more than even our family and our significant others.

The strength and quality of our friendships are better predictors of happiness and longevity, especially as we age, according to a number of Michigan State University studies. As important as our friends are to us in childhood and early adulthood, once we enter retirement age, friends can help replace the relationships we had with workplace colleagues and even assuage the loss suffered when we lose a spouse.

But not just any friend will do. We need to be careful that the friendships we cultivate are with people with whom we can relax and enjoy life. Friends who stress us out are not only less fun, they can also literally make us sick, making us more vulnerable to chronic illness. Positive, supportive friends make us happier and healthier.

The best defense is a wide circle of friends. There are fair-weather friends, who help us celebrate life's victories (but who may disappear when the going gets tough), and foul-weather friends, who give us a shoulder to cry on during bad times (but who may find it hard to be truly happy for us when things are going well). The best friends are those willing to travel life's ups and downs with us, come rain or come shine.

EXERCISE

Surprise a Friend

Sometimes we take our best friends for granted. Find a way to acknowledge your dearest friend. Surprise him or her with something wonderful the two of you can do together—a girls' night out or tickets to a ball game or concert.

The two girlfriends I've known the longest are my two best friends from high school. We live thousands of miles apart—Renée in New Orleans and Carol in Atlanta and me in New England—but we try to see each other when we can. For my 50th birthday, Carol and Renée surprised me big-time with a weekend in Las Vegas. They showed up at the airport to greet me, with signs and balloons and big smiles. Then we hung out on the Strip, and they took me to *Thunder From Down Under* one night and *Menopause The Musical* the next. We had a fabulous time.

Every time I see them I'm 16 again—and there's no friendship I treasure more.

Start planning a splendid surprise for your BFF today. You'll both live longer.

WATER BALLOON FIGHT FOR HAPPINESS

"Let the colors of Holi spread the message of
peace and happiness."
—Anonymous

In India, the Hindu celebration known as Holi, the Festival
of Colors, is a happy tradition designed to honor the joys of
spring. It's a delightful event that brings out the playful child in
everyone. People douse one another with water balloons and
toss handfuls of colored powder into the air and onto each other.
Red for love, green for abundance, orange for success, pink for
happiness. Then they indulge in a feast of desserts.

 The next time you need a little fun and frolic, invite your
friends and family over for a little Holi happiness. Lay out the
cupcakes and the brownies and the chocolate chip cookies.
Stage a water balloon fight—and don't forget the Silly String.

Call Your Mother

"Call your mother. Tell her you love her.
Remember, you're the only person who knows what her
heart sounds like from the inside."
—Rachel Wolchin

WHEN YOU'RE A CHILD, your mother is the one you run
to for a hug when you need one. (At least for most of us. If
your mother was not the nurturing sort, then swap out the
word mother here for the person who gave you the care and
consolation you needed when you needed it.) Call your mother
for comfort when you're anxious or upset, and your cortisol level
(stress hormone) is likely to drop while your oxytocin level (feel-
good hormone) rises, according to a University of Wisconsin-
Madison study.

When you're the mother on the receiving end, you may find
phone and texting interactions with your adult children to be a
mixed bag. According to a University of Texas at Austin study,
half of the phone calls and text exchanges with adult children

leave parents feeling anxious or worried. In-person visits tend to be more satisfying.

Which is no reason not to call your mother.

When I lived far away from my folks, I Skyped them often so I could see as well as hear them. (Because any day you see your mother's face—or your father's—is a good day, at least for me.) Now that we all live together, I see them most every day. Pretty sweet.

Note to Mothers Everywhere: One of the best ways to help keep your interactions with your adult children positive is to refrain from offering unsolicited advice. I know, I know—harder than it sounds. But you can do it.

You've only got one mother. Call her if you can.

EXERCISE

YOLO Mom

When we're all grown up, we feel all grown up most of the time. Except maybe when we talk to our mothers. That's not necessarily a bad thing. As we've seen, talking to our mothers on a regular basis can make us happier and healthier. It's good for moms, too, who benefit from contact with adult children.

The challenges to establishing and maintaining regular contact with our mothers and adult children can be tough, however, given the demands of our 24/7 world and how far apart many of us live from family. This may be particularly true of parents and their millennial children, according to a University of Kansas study. Millennials are digital natives, yet their parents and grandparents tend to resist using new technologies. This can handicap efforts to maintain close ties.

Get over it. The most successful communication happens when we use at least three channels at our disposal, apart from real-time visits: landline phones, cell phones, texting, instant messaging, Snapchat, email, video calls, social networking sites, etc.

I resisted texting until I realized that my youngest child, a laconic millennial, preferred that channel—unlike my older children, who were happy to use the phone and email. If I want to talk to my millennial, I text. I'm the queen of emojis now, much to his dismay.

My young grandchildren and I do yoga and make faces and chat on Skype between visits.

Note: My own mother, in her 80s, has mastered Skype just so she can see her grandchildren and great-grandchildren and interact with them as often as possible.

Add a communication channel today. Find the one that works best for you; use it often. Your mother—and your kids—deserve it.

Kiss Babies,
Shake Hands,
Embrace Strangers

"The hands of those I meet are dumbly eloquent to me.
The touch of some hands is an impertinence. I have met
people so empty of joy that when I clasped their frosty
fingertips, it seemed as if I were shaking hands with a
northeast storm. Others there are whose hands have
sunbeams in them, so that their grasp warms my heart."
—Helen Keller

CONNECTING WITH PEOPLE begins when you greet them.
Every culture has its own traditional greetings.

In France, you say *"bonjour"* to everyone you meet—on the
street, in shops and restaurants, everywhere. The failure to do
so is considered *très impoli*. In Japan, you bow and say *"ohayō."*
In the Marshall Islands, you greet one another by raising your
eyebrows. (I know, you're probably raising yours right now.) In
India, you fold your hands as if in prayer and say *"namaste."* In

Tibet, sticking out your tongue is considered a polite salutation. And in Greenland, you greet people with the Inuit *kunik*, by placing your nose and upper lip on their cheeks or foreheads, the better to smell them.

Wherever you are and whomever you may meet, greeting people with courtesy and congeniality in accordance with their cultural norms is critical to connecting with them—and connecting with people, as we've seen, is critical to our happiness.

EXERCISE

24-Hour Greeter

Now that many of the people we interact with during the course of the day are on their phones most of the time, it's getting more difficult to connect organically with people we already know, much less people we're meeting for the first time. It's easier just to brush it off and mind your own business and go back to your own phone.

Don't.

Studies published in the *Journal of Experimental Social Psychology* reveal that the ubiquitous use of phones distracts us during our face-to-face interactions with one another—and not in a good way. We enjoy hanging out with our friends and family less when smartphones are around.

For the next 24 hours, greet everyone you meet with a smile, a salutation, a handshake, a kiss, a hug—whatever is most appropriate. Don't let the presence of smartphones deter you. Connect.

G is for Gratitude

"A grateful heart is a beginning of greatness. It is
an expression of humility. It is a foundation for the
development of such virtues as prayer, faith, courage,
contentment, happiness, love and well-being."
—James E. Faust

A GRATEFUL HEART is a happy heart. Gratitude is an
essential aspect of happiness, encompassing an understanding
of and an appreciation for the good things in our lives. Think of
gratitude as a form of grace—indeed, that is one of its meanings
in the original Latin *gratia*—and you'll begin to realize its power.

Numerous psychology studies link gratitude with happiness,
according to Harvard Medical School. Feel grateful, and
you'll also feel more optimistic. You'll welcome and appreciate
positive experiences, develop more satisfying relationships,
survive tough times with more aplomb and even enjoy
better health.

Embrace gratitude, and you'll not only feel better about
yourself, you'll feel better about your family and friends, your

community, your circumstances, your life in general and whatever higher power (if any) you honor in this lifetime.

The best part of gratitude: It's a past, present and future kind of happy. You can focus on the good things that have happened in your past, letting the not-so-good things go. You can focus on the good things happening right now, enjoying each day more as it happens. You can even focus on the future, hoping and believing in good things to come.

EXERCISE

Keep a Gratitude Journal

One of the easiest ways to be grateful—endorsed by Oprah herself—is to keep a journal. Just jot down three things you are grateful for each day.

I do this every night when I say my prayers. I usually begin by praying for miracles large and small and wrap up with my gratitude list to bring me back to earth.

Whether you write in your gratitude journal or whisper your thanks to the stars doesn't matter. What matters is that you do it. Not only will you boost your physical, emotional and spiritual well-being, you'll also sleep better, according to *Applied Psychology: Health and Well-Being*. Do it every night for a week and see how you feel. Grateful, I'll bet.

Give

"For it is in giving that we receive."
—Francis of Assisi

IN SORT OF AN EXTREME New Year's resolution, I name my years. The Year of Writing, the Year of Yoga, the Year of the Dog, etc. I decided in December 2011 that 2012 would be the Year of Giving. Everything was going so well in my life that I thought I should spend the next year giving back. Every day, I pledged to give something away. I announced this to my friends and family as we all discussed resolutions for the new year to come. Worse, I wrote a blog about it. Then, just before Christmas, I got laid off.

This is what they mean when they say, "Life is what happens while you're busy making other plans."

So now I was in the awkward position of having no income and no job and no job prospects and, even more mortifying, having to ask people for help in rectifying this awkward situation—job leads, references, freelance work, etc. All this during my so-called Year of Giving.

I learned a lot that year. I learned who my friends were—and how generous they were. I also learned there are numerous ways to give: I gave away books and clothes and shoes. (OK, a lot of shoes.) I gave away essays and consultations and critiques, yoga classes and chakra workshops and massages, baked goods and casseroles, heirlooms and antiques. You name it, I gave it away.

But even 365 days of giving couldn't come close to what I received. By the time the year was over, I had a new career, a new book contract, a new attitude, a new life.

And not nearly as many pairs of shoes.

EXERCISE

The Month of Giving

Giving is a guaranteed way to make you—and the recipient—feel good. The more you give, the better you feel—and the more you give.

One of the best ways to increase giving is to boost the positive reinforcement you get whenever you give—that "helper's high" we've talked so much about. According to a study published in the *International Journal of Happiness and Development*, when we give to people we know or to organizations in which people we know are involved, we're happier than when we give to people or organizations with whom we have no social connection. We don't necessarily give less, but we enjoy the giving more.

Resolve to give away one thing a day for a month. Focus on those people and organizations with whom you have a connection. If the month goes well, try for a year. You and your closets will rejoice.

Love

"There is only one happiness in this life,
to love and be loved."
—George Sand

IT SEEMS ONLY FITTING that the last entry in this Happier Heart section should be "Love." We've explored many ways of opening your heart, and the most direct way is simply to love.

According to a Harvard study, happiness is love. That is, the people who are happiest are the people with the most loving relationships.

From the day we're born, our capacity to love and be loved profoundly affects our mental, emotional and physical health. According to studies reported by *Time*:

- Love reduces cortisol levels.
- Love boosts levels of oxytocin, dopamine and norepinephrine.
- Love helps us overcome anxiety and depression.
- Love reduces inflammation and boosts immunity.
- Love even helps relieve physical pain. In one Stanford

University study, simply looking at a picture of a loved one reduced moderate pain by 40 percent—and severe pain by 10 to 15 percent.

All of the above helps keep our hearts healthy as well as happy. Because love really is the best medicine.

EXERCISE

Love is a Verb

Making sure the loved ones in our lives know how much we care for them is an ongoing challenge. It's easy to take each other for granted. Here are some time-honored ways to show your affection and appreciation for those you love most:

Food. Every mom knows food is love. Whenever we get together as a family, my mother, the baker, makes everyone their favorite dessert: cheesecake for Greg, Rice Krispy treats for Mikey, coffee cake for Alexis, sugar-free blueberry pie for Dad, pecan pie for me. It's an embarrassment of riches and calories.

Flowers. When I was a teenager, I had a boyfriend who brought me a daisy a day. Just like the song. We moved away and I lost touch with him over the years. To this day, whenever I see a daisy, I think of him.

Chores. My uncle used to take the family car to get washed every Saturday so it would be clean for Sunday. That was his gift to my aunt, who would drive to church in the clean car and then come home in time to make a splendid Sunday dinner. He didn't go to church, but he always came to dinner.

Time. When I was a child, fathers were not generally called upon to spend much time with their children—especially their daughters. But I spent every Saturday with my father. He'd take me to work with him or on walks through the woods with the dogs. He taught me to swim and to ride a horse and to shoot with a bow and arrow.

There are all kinds of ways to show your love for your family and friends. Find what works for you and for them. Small gestures count—and over time they add up to lasting love.

---------------•• HAPPY PILLS ••---------------

Your Heart's Desire: Vitamin D

Vitamin D is known as the sunshine vitamin since your body makes it whenever your skin is exposed to sunlight. It's critical to strong bones because it helps your body process calcium. But healthy vitamin D levels are important to the rest of your body as well—and if you avoid sun, are a vegan or suffer from dairy allergies, you may not be getting enough. Vitamin D deficiency is linked to a number of health problems—from rickets and osteoporosis to asthma, cancer and depression, most notably SAD. What's more, vitamin D may help treat and prevent diabetes, hypertension, glucose intolerance and multiple sclerosis.

But the most dramatic role vitamin D may play in our health and happiness has to do with our heart. Too little of the sunshine vitamin has long been associated with cardiovascular disease. But new research from Ohio University indicates vitamin D treatment may help prevent scar tissue that can make it harder for the heart to pump blood in the wake of a heart attack.

In other words, vitamin D helps heal broken hearts.

Here's a list of good sources of vitamin D.

- Sunlight
- Fatty fish (tuna, mackerel and salmon)
- Beef liver
- Cheese
- Egg yolks
- Foods fortified with vitamin D (some dairy products, orange juice, soy milk and cereals)

(8)
Happier in Good Times

———

"Hug and kiss whoever helped get you—
financially, mentally, morally, emotionally—to
this day. Parents, mentors, friends, teachers.
If you're too uptight to do that, at least
do the old handshake thing, but I recommend
a hug and a kiss. Don't let the sun go down
without saying thank you to someone, and
without admitting to yourself that
absolutely no one gets this far alone."
—Stephen King

———

Being happy in good times can be harder than it sounds. We all know people who have everything, whose good luck and hard work and insert-appropriate-noun-here have brought them all that anyone could possibly want—and more. And yet they're miserable.

Being rich does not buy happiness. Being famous does not buy happiness. Being beautiful does not buy happiness. Yet we live in a culture that worships fame and fortune and beauty—and promises us happiness should we achieve any combination thereof.

A series of University of Rochester studies bear this out. When we know what we want and reach what we want, it doesn't necessarily make us any happier. In fact, when we get what we want, we are often less happy than we were when we started out.

Whether achieving our goals brings us satisfaction and contentment depends on what those goals are. When those goals are associated with material gain and physical attractiveness and celebrity, achieving them not only makes us unhappy, it can actually make us ill. We may suffer both psychologically and physically, due to feelings of anxiety and anger and even shame.

Setting goals that revolve around professional growth, self-realization, relationships and community are far more likely to make us happy, increasing our satisfaction with life in general and our personal fulfillment and well-being in particular—and in a big way.

In short: Be careful what you want.

And when you get it, make sure it makes you happy and fulfilled. We'll explore how to do just that in Happier in Good Times.

Be Humble

"With pride, there are many curses. With humility,
there come many blessings."
—Ezra Taft Benson

WHEN EVERYTHING IS GOING YOUR WAY, there's a
temptation to attribute that to the holy trinity of me, myself and
I. Holding on to your humility can be tough, especially in today's
"all about me" culture. And it really is all about me—we are a
society in which narcissism is on the rise, according to a study
reported in *Psychological Science*.

Humility provides a counterbalance to this extreme
individualism. The underrated value is key to your happiness,
shielding you from yourself by:

- Strengthening your relationships, allowing you to
  remain close to the people you care about at home and
  at work, even as your star rises
- Mitigating the negative effects of competitiveness,
  so that you can retain your competitive edge without
  alienating your peers

- Minimizing conflict in your relationships, alleviating stress and contributing to your good health and well-being

So, as my father would say, "Get off your high horse."

EXERCISE

Write a Fan Letter

No matter how smart or rich or pretty or talented or famous you may be, there's always someone smarter, richer, prettier, more talented or more famous than you. Identify those people. Study them, learn how they've survived the ups and downs of life and remained humble in the face of such success. If they haven't remained humble, note that too.

Now write fan letters to your top two. Detail your admiration for them in no fewer than 300 words. Be sure to reference not only the virtues that led to their successes but their resiliency and humility in overcoming their failures. Then send those fan letters.

Empathize

"True contentment comes with empathy."
—Tim Finn

THE ABILITY TO EMPATHIZE—putting yourself in someone else's shoes—is not a given. As human beings, we are by definition egocentric. Fortunately for humanity, however, the right supramarginal gyrus in our brain is programmed to detect a lack of empathy—and correct for that. When this part of our brain malfunctions and fails to autocorrect for empathy, our ability to empathize is wildly compromised, according to a study published in the *Journal of Neuroscience*.

Even when our brains are functioning properly, the greater the discrepancy between our own circumstances and other people's, the harder it is for us to empathize with those people. If we're living large and enjoying all of life's creature comforts, it's far more difficult for us to put ourselves in the shoes of people down on their luck.

The good news is the neuroplasticity of our brains allows us to reinforce the neural networks that autocorrect for empathy. Our capacity for empathy is not fixed—and practice does make perfect. Research shows some of the most effective ways to practice empathy and compassion are loving-kindness meditation, strenuous physical exercise and volunteerism.

EXERCISE

Loving-Kindness Meditation

Sit in a comfortable position, either cross-legged on the floor or in a chair that supports your back, hands folded on your lap or on your knees. Breathe in and out, deeply and slowly. Relax. When you're feeling calm and centered, you're ready to begin.

Focus on yourself. Imagine yourself at your happiest and healthiest, think good thoughts about yourself, and shower yourself with sweet blessings. Wish yourself well. If you'd like, you can use a mantra: *May I be happy. May I be healthy. May I be free from suffering.* And so on.

Focus on your loved ones. Picture their faces, imagine them at their happiest and healthiest, and send them good thoughts and sweet blessings. Wish them well. *May you be happy. May you be healthy. May you be free from suffering.*

Focus on someone with whom you are having difficulty. Someone who irritates you, frustrates you, angers you. Frenemies, enemies, etc. Picture their faces, imagine them at their happiest and healthiest, and send them good thoughts and sweet blessings. Wish them well. *May you be happy. May you be healthy. May you be free from suffering.*

Finally, focus on all living beings. Send them good thoughts and sweet blessings. Wish them well. *May all living beings be happy. May all living beings be healthy. May all living beings be free from suffering.*

This four-step loving-kindness meditation on a regular basis will help you rewire your brain for ultimate empathy and compassion.

Share

---

*"Happiness quite
unshared can scarcely
be called happiness;
it has no taste."*
—Charlotte Brontë

ANYONE WHO'S EVER ADMONISHED a child to share a toy with a pal or sibling knows that learning to share is a big deal. And we all know grown-ups who never seemed to learn how to share at all.

I was an only child and never really had to share anything with anyone unless we had company. Which was fine by me since I knew those kids would eventually have to go home and I'd have everything all to myself again. Life was good.

I grew up and had two kids 18 months apart, and they fought over everything. I didn't know what to do. When my mother-in-law made a cake and then instructed one child to cut two pieces and the other to choose the first piece, I was stunned by her genius.

When we've worked hard for our success, it can be hard to share the spoils. Or to at least feel we are worthy of the bigger piece of cake.

A study reported in *Psychological Science* shows this. When children as young as 3 years old work together for a reward, they tend to share that reward without complaint. The same is not true when they are not working together, leading researchers to believe that an innate sense of fairness rules this sharing behavior: since the toddlers both worked for it, they should share the treats.

When we remember that we did not achieve our success on our own—that we have others to thank for our good fortune—we should find it easier to share the benefits of that good fortune.

It's only fair.

EXERCISE

Share Yourself

We've all heard the saying: "Give a man a fish, and you feed him for a day; teach a man to fish and you feed him for the rest of his life."

That sounds good in theory, but considering that this man must be really hungry by now, the better thing to do would be to feed him a fish, assuage his hunger and then, when he can think straight, teach him to fish.

When was the last time you gave a man a fish and/or taught a man to fish?

My son, the philosophy major, ended up back home after college— without a job and without a plan and without a clue what to do next.

I told him he could stay as long as he needed, and I'd teach him to do the only thing I knew how to do: write. (If I'd been a plumber, I would have taught him to plumb.) I helped him come up with a book idea and I helped him pitch it to a publisher, and six months later he had written a book: *The Little Book of Bathroom Philosophy: Daily Wisdom from the World's Greatest Thinkers*. That was a decade ago and now he's written a dozen books, two films and lots of stand-up routines. He no longer lives at home.

Find yourself a hungry man, feed him and teach him to fish.

Donate

———

"Giving is not just about making a donation,
it's about making a difference."
—Kathy Calvin

———

WHEN BILL GATES WAS A YOUNG BILLIONAIRE, he
used to say he was going to spend the first half of his life making
money and the second half of his life giving it away. This led
his critics to wonder out loud just how long Gates thought he
was going to live. Then, at age 38, he married Melinda, and
together through their foundation they have given away billions
of dollars, most notably to initiatives in health care, education,
technology and more.

We're not all billionaires, but we can donate our time and
energy and effort and money to the good causes of our choice—
especially in good times. A failure to do so is not only bad for our
soul, it's bad for our happiness and well-being.

But those of us who enjoy greater wealth are not necessarily
more generous than our less well-heeled peers. In fact,

according to the National Center for Charitable Statistics, the poorest and the richest among us tend to contribute a higher percentage of income than those of us who fall in the middle. People making between $100,000 and $200,000 a year give 2.6 percent of their income, lower than the 3.6 percent people making less than $100,000 a year give, and lower than the 3.1 percent that those making more than $200,000 a year. Note: The median income is around $45,000, according to the Bureau of Labor Statistics.

Yes, you read that right. Most of us make under a hundred grand per year—and yet are more generous than our richer neighbors.

Long story short: If you're doing well, you need to step up. We all do.

EXERCISE

Choose a New Charity

How we spend our money is as critical to our happiness as how much money we make, studies suggest. When we spend money on ourselves, we aren't any happier as a result—but when we spend money on others or charitable causes, we experience a surge in happiness. This holds true no matter how much money we make.

Like you, I could always be counted on to support my favorite nonprofits, in my case, local PBS and NPR stations, the Red Cross, Goodwill and the Salvation Army. But when I wrote the first novel in my K-9 mystery series, *A Borrowing of Bones*, I did a lot of research on working dogs, notably bomb-sniffing dogs in the military and search-and-rescue dogs in law enforcement. I added organizations such as Mission K9 Rescue, which rescues and finds forever homes for abandoned military working dogs, to my donation list. Giving to these dog-saving charities makes me feel good.

Find a new charity to support with your hard-earned dollars. Make it something that matters to you in a very personal way. Give generously— and you'll feel good too.

--------------------------| HAPPY PILLS |---------------------------

Iron: Strong Enough to Care

Being strong enough to care speaks to a physical strength
as well as an emotional strength. For that we need iron—and
we're not talking metaphorically. Iron plays a critical role in our
health, and not just to produce red blood cells and transport
oxygen. It helps strengthen our muscles, boost our energy
levels and metabolism, regulate our body temperature, improve
our brain function, bolster our immunity and synthesize our
neurotransmitters. Iron is used to treat anemia, chronic diseases
of the intestinal and excretory system, and even restless leg
syndrome. It also helps us concentrate and get enough sleep.
Too little iron, and your mental, physical and emotional well-
being suffers. Worse, you run the risk of fatigue, weakness, mood
swings, depression and apathy.

Iron helps you feel strong—strong enough to care about
yourself and others.

Here are some good sources of iron:

- Fortified oatmeal
- Soybeans
- Lentils
- Red meat
- Turkey (dark meat)

Tell the Truth

"Be impeccable with your word.
Speak with integrity. Say only what you mean.
Avoid using the word to speak against yourself or
to gossip about others. Use the power of your
word in the direction of truth and love."
—Don Miguel Ruiz

MY FRIEND JOHN AND I have had a long-running argument about this question: If we could all read each other's minds, would the world be a better place? My friend John says yes, because we'd all know what we're thinking all the time. We'd know the truth. I say no, because you really don't want to know what I am thinking half the time. You—and I—can't handle the truth.

Everybody lies. A University of Massachusetts study found that 60 percent of us can't even get through a 10-minute conversation without lying. Other surveys found that 90 percent of us lie on online dating profiles (you *so* know that's true), 40 percent of us lie on our résumés and 30 percent of us lie about having seen *The Godfather*. Seriously.

Sometimes we lie so we're not found out. Sometimes we lie so we can avoid conflict or spare someone's feelings or simply not to be the bearer of bad news. Sometimes we lie to protect ourselves; sometimes we lie to protect others. Sometimes we lie just for the hell of it.

But every time we lie, we compromise our integrity. Not to mention postpone the inevitable.

As a literary agent, I'm often in the position of delivering bad news: No, I don't think this story is ready to shop; no, I can't be your agent; no, your book didn't sell, etc. No. No. No.

It's the hardest part of the job and the one I've struggled with the most—until I read this somewhere: Tell the hard truth with a kind heart. Now when I have to deliver bad news, I don't procrastinate or equivocate or prevaricate. I just tell the truth as kindly as I can.

EXERCISE

24 Hours of Truth

Tell the truth, the whole truth and nothing but the truth for the next 24 hours. No lies by omission, no half-truths and no little white lies.

When your best friend asks you if you like her new haircut or her new apartment or her boyfriend, tell the truth. When your significant other asks you if you like his friends or his barbecued ribs or his mother, tell the truth. When anyone asks you anything at all, tell the truth.

Remember: You may as well tell the truth—and not just because the truth will come out. According to a study published in *Social Psychology and Personality Science*, the most trusting among us are also the ones best able to spot a lie.

Put Money in its Rightful Place

"Money is human happiness in the abstract; and so the man who is no longer capable of enjoying such happiness in the concrete, sets his whole heart on money."
—Arthur Schopenhauer

YOU KNOW THE OLD JOKE: Money may not buy happiness, but better rich and unhappy than poor and unhappy. Which is sort of true as it turns out, according to a Princeton University study. The more money you make, the happier you are—up to an income of about $75,000 a year.

Below that threshold, you may not be sad, exactly, but you're likely to feel burned out by the struggle to make enough money.

Above that threshold, more money does not necessarily mean more happiness. The study defined two kinds of happiness, the first associated with how well our day is going (our mood) and the second associated with how well our life is going (our satisfaction with our place in the world). How much money we make influences the second kind of happiness, but it has little bearing on the first. Moreover, the wealthier we are, the less we are able to enjoy what our wealth can buy us, according to studies reported in *Psychological Science.*

We've all heard the stories of lottery winners who lose it all in record time. According to the National Endowment for Financial Education, a whopping 70 percent of people who find themselves wealthy overnight lose their newfound fortunes within a few years. Many experience divorce and substance abuse, along with bankruptcy; some fall victim to scam artists, suicide and even murder.

If you do come into a sudden windfall, get a financial advisor, beware of too-good-to-be-true investments, curb your spending, make few financial commitments and decide in advance which family, friends and charities you are willing to help and to what degree you are willing to help them. Finding a way to make peace with your monetary success is important. Understand that money is just money—a tool—not a panacea.

The trick to building wealth and a happy life? Focus on the happy life part and not the wealth part. By this far into this book, you're figuring out how to do that.

EXERCISE

The Happy Millionaire

Let's say you have a million dollars. If you really do, great. If not, pretend you do. If you're thinking, well, a million dollars isn't very much anymore, especially if you live in New York City or California or wherever it costs a million bucks just to buy a little house, then make it 2 million. But no more than that.

Create a list of all your financial goals and bucket list items: pay off the mortgage, build a nest egg for retirement, establish a college fund, buy a second home, take a trip around the world, buy your mother a car, etc.

Now attach a dollar figure to each of those goals.

See how fast that million dollars disappears.

What has this told you about your attitude toward money? Your spending habits? Your wishlist?

Give Back

"It is every man's obligation to put
back into the world at least the equivalent
of what he takes out of it."
—Albert Einstein

ONE OF THE BEST WAYS to avoid being a jerk when you're flying high is to give back. Giving back not only reminds you where you came from, it reminds you how it feels to be stuck on the ground when all you want to do is soar through the sky. And that without the wind beneath your wings, you wouldn't be up there now.

Giving back gives us a purpose beyond our own immediate interests. As we've seen, people with a sense of purpose are happier; it's good for our physical, emotional and mental health, our longevity, even our genes. We even sleep better at night according to a study from *Sleep Science and Practice*.

Lee Child, No. 1 *New York Times* bestselling author of the *Jack Reacher* series, is rich and handsome and wildly successful. He writes a book a year, year in and year out. Yet no one in publishing is more generous when it comes to giving back. He's known for reading and endorsing his fellow writers' books—and I don't mean just big-name authors like himself. He blurbs the novels of unknown newcomers too; he even blurbed my debut mystery, *A Borrowing of Bones*. "A compelling mix of hard edges and easy charm," he said—words which will grace my tombstone. Child remembers what it was like to be a debut novelist trying to get read. So he gives back. He's the rich and famous writer we should all grow up to be.

EXERCISE

The Boomerang

Think of a kindness someone has done you in the past. How have you thanked them? How have you given back?

At one point during my very unhappy first marriage, I found myself miles away from my family and friends, alone in a big house out in the cornfields with the babies and no husband in sight. My childhood friend Renée called and knew in a minute how miserable I was. She sent me a ticket to New Orleans to visit her. (There's nothing like a trip to New Orleans to raise your spirits.) I returned the favor a couple of years later, when she needed to get away from her life for a while. A boomerang gift.

Give someone in your life a boomerang gift. Happiness will come right back to you.

Pay it Forward

―――――

"If you can't pay it back, pay it forward."
—Catherine Ryan Hyde

―――――

SOMETIMES THE PEOPLE WHO helped us the most are not around by the time we make it. Or if they are, we've lost touch and can't find them. Or maybe we never knew who they were.

The grandmother who bequeathed us the tuition for medical school. The coach who encouraged us to run faster, jump higher, throw farther. The librarian who let us into the adult reading section long before we'd reached the prescribed age. The stranger who bought us a bus ticket when we really, really needed to get home. So we pay it forward.

David Rosenfelt and Carolyn Haines are two animal lovers who walk the talk. Both are successful writers whose books feature dogs and cats. Each has started a charity devoted to caring for needy animals. Rosenfelt runs the Tara Foundation, a dog rescue named in honor of "the greatest golden retriever the world has ever known." Four thousand rescued dogs and counting. Haines runs the Good Fortune Farm Refuge, a nonprofit ranch where she rehabilitates abused and abandoned animals and finds homes for rescued animals.

They're paying it forward in honor of the animals that inspire the four-legged characters that grace their novels. Just thinking about them makes me want to go rescue another dog (or two) or cat (or two). Which is the point.

EXERCISE

Forward Times Three

Catherine Ryan Hyde wrote the book *Pay It Forward*, inspired by the two strangers who rescued her from a burning car and then disappeared before she could thank them. In her novel, a 12-year-old boy comes up with a pay-it-forward networking plan for a school project, in which someone done a favor must do three favors for three other people.

Think of a favor someone has done for you. Now find a way to pay it forward with three favors you do for other people. Explain to those you help that they should pay it forward too. See how far your own networking plan may go—and where it may lead you.

Be Aware

"Look at everything always as though
you were seeing it either for the first or last time:
Thus is your time on earth filled with glory."
—Betty Smith

SELF-AWARENESS IS A VERY DESIRABLE yet elusive quality that benefits us in so many ways. Research shows self-awareness breeds confidence, creativity and communication skills. When we see ourselves clearly, we enjoy better relationships, make better decisions and perform more effectively. We are even less likely to lie, cheat and steal.

However, few of us are as self-aware as we think we are. A study reported in the *Harvard Business Review* revealed that while most of us think we're self-aware, only 10 to 15 percent of us actually are. Worse, the more experienced and powerful we are, the harder it may be for us to see ourselves clearly and the more likely we are to think overly well of ourselves.

The study identified two kinds of self-awareness:

Internal self-awareness is how well we understand

ourselves, from our values and behaviors to our thoughts and feeling and reactions. When we have high internal self-awareness, we enjoy greater personal and professional fulfillment. We're happier.

External self-awareness is how well we understand how other people see us and feel about us. When we have high external self-awareness, we're better at putting ourselves in other people's shoes and understanding their points of view. We're happier in our relationships.

EXERCISE

Benjamin Franklin's T-Chart

You may have heard of Benjamin Franklin's famous T-chart, which he used to weigh the pros and cons of a given situation before making important decisions. People still use that T-chart today, especially salespeople, who have dubbed it the "Ben Franklin close."

What you may not know—at least I didn't—was that Franklin also used the T-chart as a balance sheet to help him address his own strengths and weaknesses. He noted his strengths in one column, not only the ones he felt he already had but also those he wished to cultivate. In the other column, he listed his weaknesses. This helped him track his character growth over time—a self-awareness technique of the first order.

Make a balance sheet for your strengths and weaknesses. Track your progress, so you see how your self-awareness improves—along with your character—over time.

AROUND THE WORLD IN HAPPY WAYS

HEAVEN AND HELL

There's an old Zen story about the nature of self-awareness:

A samurai warrior, impatient for enlightenment, confronts a Zen master while the monk is deep in meditation. He yells at the Zen master, bellowing, "Tell me the nature of heaven and hell." The Zen master opens his eyes, tossing a flurry of insults the warrior's way.

Enraged, the samurai draws his sword and raises it above the monk's head.

"That is hell," says the monk.

The warrior lowered his sword to the ground, understanding that he had created his own hell of anger and hatred. He folded his hands in the prayer position, bowing to the Zen master.

"That is heaven," said the monk.

This parable has been shared among Buddhists countless times for countless generations—and its relevance still resonates today.

———

"Plant your garden and decorate your own soul, instead of waiting for someone to bring you flowers."
—Jorge Luis Borges

———

(9)

Happier in Bad Times

"Perhaps all the dragons in our lives
are princesses who are only waiting
to see us act, just once, with
beauty and courage."
—Rainer Maria Rilke

Holding on to happiness during tough times is not easy. And yet all of us must face trials and tribulations sooner or later. None of us get through this life free of pain or suffering. As John Irving says in *The World According to Garp*, "we are all terminal cases."

But that doesn't mean we can't be happy. Even when life throws challenges at us—as it inevitably does—we can face those challenges with strength and adaptability.

You've heard of PTSD, post-traumatic stress disorder. But at the other end of the spectrum is a phenomenon called post-traumatic growth, where you find meaning and wisdom in the trauma you suffer, setting the stage for significant personal growth that transforms your life in a deep and profound way.

This demands a psychological flexibility that is critical to our well-being, according to a study published in the *Clinical Psychology Review*. When we acknowledge our emotions and allow ourselves to feel them, we can learn to handle our distress better—and in so doing, move from pain to transcendence.

How happy we are depends more on the way we react to what happens to us, rather than what actually happens to us. Bad times come and go; the bad feelings that accompany bad times come and go too. Just because we're miserable today doesn't mean we'll be miserable tomorrow.

With the right tools, we can survive and thrive even in the worst of times.

Because happiness isn't about being happy all the time.

Have Faith

———

"Faith is what makes life bearable, with all its tragedies
and ambiguities and sudden, startling joys."
—Madeleine L'Engle

———

THERE ARE TIMES IN LIFE when we are tested so severely
that even the most optimistic and spiritual among us suffer a
crisis of faith—in ourselves, in each other, in whatever power we
believe in. During The Worst Year of My Life—which began with
losing my man, my job and (nearly) my child, and ended with
9/11—I spent a lot of time driving around in my silver Saturn
on the freeways of Silicon Valley yelling at God. Personally, I'd
always been a glass-half-full, prayerful kind of person who kept
it together through thick and thin thanks to what I saw as an
indefatigable combination of grit
and grace.

Not so indefatigable, as it turned out. I was burned out on
love, burned out on life and burned out on God. I had to find my
way back—and that started with finding my way back to spirit.

Finding our way back to faith is critical to our happiness. Multiple studies have long revealed that people of faith are happier than nonbelievers—and that people of faith who are part of a spiritual community are happier still. What's more, going to church or synagogue or mosque or temple on a regular basis gives us a support system—both communal and spiritual—that helps us handle tough times better, according to a study by the Austin Institute for the Study of Family and Culture.

EXERCISE

Group Hug and a Prayer

Go to a service. If you already go to your local church, synagogue, mosque, Buddhist temple, Quaker meeting house or insert-spiritual-center-of-your-choice-here, then good for you. If you don't, that's fine too. What matters is that you reconnect with your spirit and whatever higher power you pray to—be it Jesus or Yahweh or the energy of the universe—and that you do it in the company of others.

If you don't know anyone you can join for a service or you feel uncomfortable doing so, take a cue from the Japanese. In Japan, people are long on spiritual tradition—from Shinto and Buddhism to Christianity—and short on dogma. Their ecumenical approach allows them to celebrate holidays together in community.

You, too, can take an ecumenical approach. Go to mass with a Catholic colleague; attend a temple with a Buddhist friend, celebrate Shabbat Friday night dinner at the house of Jewish friends; etc. Have a group hug and a prayer and—all together now—an "amen."

Beef up Your Resiliency

"There were many dark moments when my faith in humanity was sorely tested, but I would not and could not give myself up to despair. That way lays defeat and death."
—Nelson Mandela

WHEN I WAS A KID and something bad happened to me, the Colonel would say, "Adversity builds character." What my father meant by that was: Fix it or forget it. Regardless, get on with it. Be resilient.

Years later, after having gone through a particularly difficult ordeal, I told my dad about it, and he expressed dismay on my behalf. I reminded him that adversity builds character. He said, "You've got enough character."

That's hands down the nicest thing he's ever said to me.

Resiliency is more than getting back up when life knocks us down. It's getting up, moving on and growing stronger and wiser from the experience. Fortunately, we can learn resilience. Martin Seligman, known as the father of positive psychology, has created resiliency training used by therapists. This training focuses on developing our:

- Self-awareness
- Self-regulation
- Mental agility
- Character strengths
- Connection
- Optimism

All these qualities are, as we've seen, associated with happy brains, happy bodies and happy hearts. As resilient people, we exhibit all of these qualities—and as a result we are happier.

EXERCISE

Emotion Journal

Part of being resilient is emotional intelligence. When we are emotionally intelligent, we can identify and understand our own emotions as well as those of our fellow humans. That understanding informs our thought processes and behavior, helping us function better at work and at home.

We can start by practicing our emotional intelligence. Keep an emotional journal, in which you jot down the emotions you experience each day — and the triggers for those emotions. Do the same thing for the people with whom you interact. This will train you to be more sensitive to your own emotional state and that of others as well.

If you're thinking "piece of cake," think again. A study published in the *Proceedings of the National Academy of Sciences* identified many emotions in addition to the classic six of happiness, sadness, anger, surprise, fear and disgust:

- Admiration
- Adoration
- Aesthetic appreciation
- Amusement
- Anxiety
- Awe
- Awkwardness
- Boredom
- Calmness
- Confusion
- Contempt
- Craving
- Disappointment
- Empathetic pain
- Entrancement
- Envy
- Excitement
- Guilt
- Horror
- Interest
- Joy
- Nostalgia
- Pride
- Relief
- Romance
- Satisfaction
- Sexual desire
- Sympathy
- Triumph

Boost Your Self-Care

"Almost everything will work again if you unplug
it for a few minutes, including you."
—Anne Lamott

DURING THE WORST YEAR OF MY LIFE, my older children
came to visit me and my youngest, Mikey, and we went to the
mall. I was suffering crying bouts at the time, mostly at night
after Mikey was in bed. I was already unsteady; having all my
kids together completely unmoored me.

I cried at the mall. I scared my children. I went to my doctor.
When I asked her why I was falling apart now, during what was
admittedly a terrible time but not nearly as terrible as others I'd
survived with more aplomb earlier in my life, she said, "We all
have a saturation point. You have reached yours."

We all have our saturation points—and when we hit them,
it feels like crystals are growing in our heads, just like in those

saturation point experiments with sugar crystals we did in science class in grade school.

That's when it's time for a little self-care. This means slowing down, listening to your mind and body and spirit, and doing whatever you have to do to restore, refresh and reinvigorate yourself.

EXERCISE

Self-Care 101

When we're having a bad day or a bad month or a bad life, we may find it hard to pierce the fog of disappointment and despair long enough to take good care of ourselves. That's why it's good to establish the habit of self-care right here, right now, no matter what your circumstances.

Outline the things you do (or would like to do) that qualify as self-care. Here's a list to get you started:

- Massages
- Yoga
- Exercise
- Aromatherapy

- Naps
- Retreats
- Spa days
- Vacations

- Movie night
- Dinner with friends
- Road trips
- Time in nature

Incorporate at least one of these into your weekly schedule. You heard me, write "nap" every day right into your calendar. And do it now.

Whenever you're feeling weary or whiny or depressed or stressed, pull out your list and add more self-care activities to your calendar. You deserve it.

Hone Your Sense of Humor

"A keen sense of humor helps us to overlook the unbecoming, understand the unconventional, tolerate the unpleasant, overcome the unexpected and outlast the unbearable."
—Billy Graham

LAUGHTER IS THE BEST MEDICINE. We've all heard this a million times, but in many ways it's true. Study after study confirms that humor is one of the best defenses against unhappiness and one of the most reliable indicators of happiness. When we laugh, our hearts and bodies and brains experience the same benefits we get when we exercise—decreasing stress, lowering blood pressure, enhancing our immune system, boosting endorphin levels and flooding our brains with dopamine, according to a Loma Linda University study. Laughter can also improve our short-term memory and help us deal with the grief we suffer at the loss of a loved one.

Humor can be especially helpful in bad times. A good sense of humor helps us shrink the time we need to reframe the bad things that happen to us—and we can laugh at it sooner. Just watching a funny movie or stand-up routine when we're feeling down can provide some relief, according to the Mayo Clinic.

For best results, we need to learn to laugh not just at pratfalls and one-liners and cat videos—we need to learn to laugh at ourselves. University of Granada researchers have found that the more jokes we make at our own expense, the happier we tend to be. The study, published in *Personality and Individual Differences*, reveals that self-deprecating humor is tied to higher levels of sociability as well.

Go ahead, tell a joke. If you're the punch line, all the better.

EXERCISE

Invite a Comedian to Lunch

The Chinese have a curse: *May you live in interesting times.* I believe there's a corollary for parents: May you have interesting children.

I have interesting children, and they have enlivened and enlightened my life in myriad ways. My middle child is a comedian—no, really—and from the age of 2 he has been making me laugh. Even when I am feeling my worst, he can reduce me to tears of laughter—making fun of me, his siblings, the world at large and himself. That's the power of humor.

Who's your funniest friend? Invite that person to lunch at least once a month.

Laugh. Laugh harder. Laugh some more.

Hang on to Hope

"Hope is being able to see that there is light
despite all of the darkness."
—Desmond Tutu

HOPE IS CLOSELY RELATED to happiness; happy people
tend to be hopeful, that is, to harbor positive feelings about the
future. Hopeful people are happier, tolerate pain better and
live longer. In fact, a feeling of hopelessness can be a significant
predictor of mortality, according to studies reported in
Psychology Today.

Hope—unlike happiness—is not an emotion. It's a learned
condition, one common to most cultures and religious traditions
around the world, according to a California State University
study. You can see the hope in these proverbs:

- *However long the night, the dawn will break.*
  —AFRICAN PROVERB
- *If it were not for hope, the heart would break.*
  —GREEK PROVERB

265

- *As long as we have hope, we have direction, the energy to move and the map to move by.* —CHINESE PROVERB
- *Keep your eyes on the sun and you will not see the shadows.* —ABORIGINAL PROVERB
- *In the land of hope, there is never any winter.*
  —RUSSIAN PROVERB
- *The darkest hours are just before the dawn.*
  —ENGLISH PROVERB
- *Hope is the dream of a soul awake.* —FRENCH PROVERB

When the going gets tough, we may not be that happy but we can remain hopeful. And that hopefulness helps us weather the storms until the sun comes out and our happiness shines bright once more.

EXERCISE

Learning Hopefulness

You can learn to be more positive about your own future. These three strategies can help brighten your hopes, according to a study in *Psychology Today*:

1. Set meaningful goals for your personal and professional life.
2. Start now by making changes to your daily routine in service of those goals.
3. List several different ways to help you reach your goals. The more the merrier.

Do this, and not only will you train yourself to be more hopeful, you'll perform better. Research bears this out: Hopeful workers outperform their less optimistic colleagues. The hopeful salesperson sells more; the hopeful mortgage broker closes more loans; the hopeful exec meets corporate goals more often.

Most important: Master the art of hope, and you'll live a more meaningful and productive life. And that's a recipe for happiness.

Favor the Bold in You

"Fortune favors the bold."
—Virgil

WHEN YOU'RE DOWN AND OUT and unsure how to pull yourself up and onward, a bold move may help get you moving. There's a power in it.

When I was a 28-year-old stay-at-home mom, I found myself newly separated with two small children, a house in foreclosure, a car in repossession and an estranged husband who'd disappeared with all our money, leaving behind nothing but a pair of underwear emblazoned with the name "Jim" in gold lettering. My husband's name was not Jim.

I had no income and no job prospects. I tried for six months to find a job, armed only with an overwhelming desperation and an underwhelming résumé.

Nothing.

I was out of options—and soon to be out on the streets. Time to go big or go home, literally, and move in with my folks.

I wrote a new cover letter, one that read like a stand-up routine, outlining my extraordinary circumstances and making the point that if anyone needed a job, I did. I sent out that cover letter to more than a hundred publishers in the area.

I got one, and only one, response. It was from Tom Owens, the editor of a business magazine, who said I made him laugh. Tom hired me, even though his boss warned him no real professional would ever write a cover letter like that.

And so began my decades-long career in publishing.

EXERCISE

Go Big Now

Think about the boldest moves you could make in your life right now.

Make a list: Start a business. Move to Tokyo. Take up skydiving. Join a local theater group. Adopt a child. Walk the Appalachian Trail.

When a dear friend of mine found herself depressed and stuck in her life, she decided she needed to do something bold to blast her out of the rut. She quit her job, sold her house and moved to Paris for a year to become the writer and photographer she'd always dreamed of being. In Paris, she reconnected with her inner artist and challenged herself to be her best self—with a little French twist. It worked, and she's since published dozens of books and countless photographs—not to mention had the experience of a lifetime and even learned *un peu français* along the way.

What would you do if you had the courage? Do it now.

┌─ AROUND THE WORLD IN HAPPY WAYS ─┐

HAPPINESS, JAPANESE STYLE

In Japan, the most desirable form of happiness is *ikigai*, defined loosely as "that which fulfills you." *Ikigai*—*iki* meaning "life" and *gai* meaning "worth"—is having a reason to get up in the morning, a sort of Japanese take on *raison d'être*.

What makes *ikigai* different from our view of happiness is its focus on the future. According to a study by Michiko Kumano at Osaka Ohtani University, *ikigai* is associated not only with positive feelings and a sense of purpose and accomplishment, but also with the confidence that you can maintain those positive feelings and sense of purpose and accomplishment through good times and bad. The ability to face hardship with hope is a critical aspect of *ikigai*. This emphasis may be one of the reasons that Japan boasts one of the longest life expectancies in the world.

Live long and prosper *ikigai*!

Be Patient

"If we want to live wider and deeper lives,
not just faster ones, we have to practice patience—
patience with ourselves, with other people, and with
the big and small circumstances of life itself."
—M.J. Ryan

PATIENCE IS ONE OF THE QUIET virtues that often goes unsung. And yet the ability to tolerate frustration and adversity with equanimity is critical not only to our health but to our happiness as well. Multiple studies reported in UC Berkeley's *Greater Good Magazine* reveal that good things do indeed come to those who wait. When we practice patience, we're less vulnerable to anxiety and depression—and on the flip side, we're more empathetic, more hopeful, more generous and more forgiving. We're even more likely to vote. In short, we're happier.

Ask yourself what kind of people, places and circumstances most try your patience: the chronically late colleague, the lumbering bureaucracy of the DMV, the long obligatory slog up the career ladder. Sometimes we can outwit, outpace or outplay these infuriating people, places and circumstances, but often we cannot. The only option is to outlast them. This is where patience comes in, allowing us to make the most of a bad situation, one way or another, without endangering our health or happiness.

Remember the Buddhist saying: If you have a problem that can be fixed, then there's no point worrying about it. If you have a problem that cannot be fixed, then there's no point worrying about it.

EXERCISE

The Traffic Test

Eighty-three percent of us drive to work—and 21 percent of us find that commute stressful. We're not imagining that stress. An MIT study cites that city driving is as physically and emotionally stressful as skydiving. Not to mention the road rage that a whopping 80 percent of us experience, according to a study by the AAA Foundation for Traffic Safety.

The longer the commute and the worse the traffic, the greater the toll on our bodies and brains—leading to obesity, high blood pressure, insomnia and chronic stress levels, and putting us at risk for depression and anxiety, heart disease, diabetes, stroke and cancer.

One of the things most likely to trigger this commuter stress: impatience. The next time you drive, pay attention to your stress level. Note when you find yourself growing impatient with slowdowns, gridlock, detours, discourtesy of other drivers, noise, pollution, etc.

To keep your cool:
- Listen to relaxing music
- Practice deep breathing
- Avoid traveling with backseat drivers
- Move away from overly aggressive drivers
- Leave earlier or later
- Try another route

When my kids were little and distracted me with their bickering while I was driving, I would play Dan Millman's spiritual classic, *Way of the Peaceful Warrior.* It calmed me down and put the kids to sleep. Pronto.

Shift Your Perspective

"Some people see the glass half full.
Others see it half empty. I see a glass that's
twice as big as it needs to be."
—George Carlin

WHEN I WAS DOING MY yoga teacher training, I had trouble mastering the headstand. It wasn't that I was physically incapable of doing it. I had the strength, the control and the balance. What I didn't have was the will. The simple truth: I didn't like being upside down.

Whenever I lowered my head to the ground, cupping my skull in my interlaced hands, I was fine. But when I began to raise my legs up into the air, I'd panic. Literally. I'd have a panic attack every time I tried to stand on my head. My yoga teacher trainer asked me to consider why I didn't think I could hold myself up, but that wasn't the problem. I knew that I could hold myself up, literally and metaphorically.

The headstand is called the King of Asanas, a seminal yoga pose celebrated for its health benefits but even more prized for opening the crown chakra, the energy center that serves as the bridge to the cosmos. Enlightenment, as it were.

I needed to do it. I went to my yoga guru Emma for a private headstand class. She knew me very well and could see through my fear. "You are someone who likes everything in its place. Headstand turns you—and your world—upside down. Everything is no longer in its place. That scares you."

She was right. Once I told myself that I could survive—indeed *had* survived—a world where everything was not in its place, I learned to do a headstand. Thanks to the King of Asanas, I know that changing perspective is the key to embracing life in all its messiness.

EXERCISE

A New Perspective

When we're unhappy, the best thing we can do is turn our world upside down and take a long, hard look at life from a new perspective. This ability allows us to reframe our negative thoughts and feelings, seeing life through a new lens of gratitude and appreciation. You don't have to do a headstand to gain a new perspective (but it couldn't hurt).

The next time you find yourself unhappy about something, look around at the other people in the room. Ask yourself if you would trade troubles with any of them. The first time I was advised to do this was at a retreat where I'd gone to figure out my next move now that I'd been unceremoniously laid off. I was feeling sorry for myself. But as I looked around at my fellow retreat participants, all of whom had come to work out issues far more serious than mine—estranged children, adulterous spouses, serious health problems—I realized I had a lot to be thankful for. My perspective changed—and I went from whining about my life to counting my blessings.

Even as we find ourselves envying others and their "perfect lives," we inevitably find out their lives are not as perfect as we believed—and that we wouldn't trade our troubles for theirs.

Practice Fortitude

"Fortitude implies a firmness and strength of mind that enables us to do and suffer as we ought. It rises upon an opposition, and, like a river, swells the higher for having its course stopped."
—Jeremy Collier

FORTITUDE IS DEFINED by *Merriam-Webster* as the "strength of mind that enables a person to encounter danger or bear pain or adversity with courage."

Mind over matter—that's what fortitude is. And as such it is the well from which courage springs. Study after study reinforces the conventional wisdom that courage is a cornerstone of happiness. To put it plainly: It's hard to be scared and happy at the same time.

When we're scared, we don't act—even when action is necessary to survive and thrive. That's where fortitude comes in, giving us the courage we need to quiet our fear response, produced by the amygdala, the part of our brain associated with fear and anxiety. We can develop more fortitude by facing our fears and overcoming them.

Here's a three-step plan to fortify yourself against your fears and prime yourself for action:

1. Acknowledge the fear.

2. Embrace the fear.

3. Act on that fear.

You can do it. And you know you want to.

EXERCISE

The Fear Factor

We're all afraid of something. According to a Self Help Collective survey, our top fears are:

1. Flying	6. Death
2. Public speaking	7. Failure
3. Heights	8. Rejection
4. The dark	9. Spiders
5. Intimacy	10. Commitment

No matter what you're afraid of, you can conquer that fear—and build fortitude in the process. Whenever you find yourself resisting change, ask yourself: What's the worst that can happen?

I was once very nervous about public speaking thanks to a play I did in high school where I totally forgot my lines. The worst that could happen? Forgetting my lines again—only this time I'd be all alone up there, with no fellow players to cover for me. Once I realized that, I started preparing slideshow presentations. They give the audience something to look at and they keep me on track and talking.

Volunteer

"To ease another's heartache is to forget one's own."
—Abraham Lincoln

WHEN YOU'RE STUMBLING through your own bad time, sometimes the only way to rise above it is to help someone whose suffering exceeds your own. The easiest way to do that is to volunteer.

If you've ever applied for college or held a job, odds are you're already familiar with the benefits of volunteering in terms of career advancement—from networking and building job skills to helping you get into college or get a promotion at work. But what you may not appreciate is how good volunteering is for your physical, emotional and spiritual health.

Volunteer, and you'll not only help make life better for your fellow humans and creatures, you'll also be part of something bigger than yourself. You'll make connections, form friendships, even have fun. You'll feel less angry, anxious, depressed and stressed out—and more confident, more fulfilled and more purposeful. Happier. You'll even live longer, according to studies reported in *Social Science and Medicine.*

Find something that engages and enlightens you. Try:

- Hospitals and assisted-living centers
- Daycare centers and after-school programs
- Community theaters, museums and arts organizations
- Libraries, historical societies and monuments
- Senior centers
- Service organizations such as Red Cross, Goodwill, Lions Club, Rotary Club, etc.
- Soup kitchens, shelters, halfway houses
- Animal shelters, rescue organizations, wildlife centers
- Youth organizations, Boys & Girls Clubs, sports teams
- Historical restorations, national parks and conservation organizations
- Places of worship

EXERCISE

Stand up for a Cause

There are many ways to volunteer. You don't have to quit your job or give away all your money or join the Peace Corps (although it would be swell if you did). All you have to do is offer your talent or expertise or resources in the service of others a few hours a week. That adds up to about 100 hours a year—the optimum time in terms of the benefit for you and your cause.

The point is to enjoy the work you do, the people you do it with and the cause you do it for. Here's a checklist to help you find the perfect volunteer opportunity, as recommended by the *World Volunteer Web*. Check the ones that apply to you:

- ☐ I want to focus on helping my neighbors and community.
- ☐ I want to meet people I wouldn't meet in usual circles at work or home.
- ☐ I want to try something new.
- ☐ I want to do something meaningful with my spare time.
- ☐ I want to explore different places and cultures and societies.
- ☐ I want to acquire skills and experience that could lead to a new career.
- ☐ I want to put my interests and pastimes to good work.
- ☐ I want to do something that draws upon my skills and talents.

Reach Out

"Regardless of what challenge you are facing right
now, know that it has not come to stay.
It has come to pass. During these times, do what you
can with what you have, and ask for help if needed.
Most importantly, never surrender.
Put things in perspective. Take care of yourself.
Find ways to replenish your energy, strengthen your
faith and fortify yourself from the inside out."
—Les Brown

REACHING OUT AND ASKING FOR HELP is not easy.
Many of us balk at the very idea. Yet asking for help benefits
us in many ways, according to studies reported in *Psychology
Today*. First, when we're feeling comfortable enough to ask
someone for assistance, we are acknowledging a connection
and mutual trust. Second, getting help when we need it makes
us happy because it relieves our stress, improves our lives and
reminds us we have a support network we can count on. In the
words of Benjamin Franklin, "If you want to make a friend, let
someone do you a favor." Third, when we ask someone for help,

we boost their happiness as well as ours.

I still have a hard time accepting this. As an agent and editor and reader, I'm always plugging other people's books—clients, friends, colleagues. But when my mystery debuted, I was put in the position of asking people to plug my book. It was a very awkward ask for me. But ask I did—and the generous response has been gratifying and humbling all at once.

If you find it hard to ask for help, ask yourself why. Do you hesitate out of fear or pride or a sense of unworthiness? Give yourself permission to ask.

Happiness is a two-way street. Happy people help people when asked—and happy people ask for help when they need it. Both helper and helpee are the happier for it.

EXERCISE

Ask for Help Now

Sometimes happiness eludes us completely and the bad times threaten to overwhelm us. When we simply cannot see a way out or around or through, it's time to ask for help.

Call your mother, text your best friend, sit down and have a heart-to-heart talk with your significant other, make an appointment with your doctor.

If time is of the essence and/or you can't bring yourself to talk to anyone you know, call a therapist or 9-1-1 or a hotline, or go straight to the emergency room.

National Suicide Prevention Lifeline   1-800-273-8255
National Domestic Violence Hotline   1-800-799-SAFE (7233)

For a full list of hotlines, go here:

psychcentral.com/lib/common-hotline-phone-numbers/

For free immediate online crisis chat assistance:

contact-usa.org/chat

crisistextline.org (for your smartphone)

suicidepreventionlifeline.org/gethelp/lifelinechat.aspx

imalive.org

AROUND THE WORLD IN HAPPY WAYS

SHINRIN-YOKU: THE JAPANESE ART OF FOREST BATHING

"But I'll tell you what hermits realize. If you go off into a far, far forest and get very quiet, you'll come to understand that you're connected with everything."
—Alan Watts

As humans, we are of the trees and from the trees. The trees are our home. All that oxygen, all that green, all good for us.

The Japanese know this—and they've taken hiking to the next level. Known as *shinrin-yoku*—forest bathing—this practice is as simple as a two-hour walk in the woods. The benefits are enormous, as discovered by Japan's Forest Therapy Study Group:

- Lower blood pressure
- Less stress
- Better cardiovascular and metabolic health
- Lower blood sugar levels
- Less depression
- Better pain management
- Better concentration and memory
- Higher energy levels
- Improved immunity
- Increased anticancer protein production

Forest bathing can even help you lose weight. Get thee to a forest.

Happier Now

―――

"To be in the moment is the miracle."
—Osho

―――

ARE WE HAPPY YET? There's a version of an old Zen story the
monks like to tell. The Buddha was wandering in the wilderness.
He got lost. Eventually he came to a swiftly moving stream too
dangerous to swim across. He needed a raft. He gathered fallen
tree limbs and pulled down vines and, using the vines to bind
together the limbs, he fashioned himself a sturdy raft and made
his way across the wild waters to the other side. He went on
his way, taking the raft with him should he need it again. He
portaged the raft for days, until he could no longer detect the
river's scent on the breeze that rippled through the trees. When
he made camp that evening, he burned the raft, making a great
fire that burned through the night. The next morning, he put out
the smoldering remains and continued on his journey.

If you're thinking, so why burn the raft, why not leave it for
the next guy, good for you. They asked the Buddha why too, and
he answered: Sometimes you have to build your own raft.

When it comes to our own happiness, it is up to each of us to
build our own raft. I hope this little book has given you the tree
limbs and vines you need to help you build yours. Use it to ford

your own stream, carry it as long as you must, then burn it. Just like the Buddha, you won't need it anymore.

Sit still and close your eyes.

Inhale joy.

Exhale more joy.

Inhale peace.

Exhale more peace.

Inhale happy.

Exhale more happy.

That's all there is to it. That's the miracle of the moment.

Be here. Be here now. Be happy now.

Happier every day.

Acknowledgements

It takes a village to make a book—and it takes a happy village to make a book about happiness. I've been blessed to work with an inspiring—and inspired—group of people on this project. Notably Phil Sexton—friend, publisher, fellow writer and pursuer of happiness, who believed in me and this book from the start. Thank you, Phil.

A shout-out to everyone at Macmillan Publishers and Media Lab Books, especially Kaytie Norman, Jeff Ashworth, Benjamin VanHoose, Courtney Kerrigan, Holland Baker and Michelle Lock.

All love and gratitude to my parents, who gave me the greatest gift a daughter can ask for: a happy childhood. Any capacity I have for happiness I owe first and foremost to them. Here's hoping I've shared at least some of that joy with those who make me happiest: my children Alexis, Greg and Mikey; my grandchildren Elektra, Calypso and Demelza; Michael; Trisha and Chris; Chris, Taryn and Shelby; my godmother Susie and my cousin Tony; and all my friends and adopted family, especially Nani and Michele, who dared me to do my yoga teacher training, for which I am forever grateful.

To my spiritual teachers, past and present: the Army chaplains of my youth, Father Pat, Father Bob and Father George; Sister Esther, Sister Patrice and all the Ursuline nuns educating girls around the globe; my godfather Bo, who never stopped praying for me; Rabbi Burton E. Levinson, who shared the wisdom and tradition of Judaism with me; Father Thomas A. Kopp, the first priest in decades who could get me to Mass on Sunday; Julia Cameron and Shakti Gawain and Pema Chödrön and Krishna Das and Mark Nepo, whose enlightenment has warmed the bud of my own; Shiva Rea and Dana Flynn and Daniel Lacerda and Chip Hartranft and Daniel Aaron and all of the yogis and yoginis I've been privileged to practice with and learn from, especially everyone at Kripalu, where my yoga journey began; and last but not least, my beloved yoga teachers Emma Spencer Boyle and Michelle Fleming, to whom this book is dedicated with respect and appreciation.

Finally, a special thank you to readers here and everywhere. May you find the life, liberty and happiness you pursue—one breath at a time.

Namaste, forever and ever, amen.

About the Author

PAULA MUNIER is a writer and yoga teacher. She earned her 200-hour Certified Yoga Teacher Credential in Transformational Yoga from Sanctuary Studios in Plymouth, Massachusetts. She's also certified to teach Senior Yoga, Pranayama and Paddleboard Yoga. She teaches chakra and mindfulness workshops in addition to asana classes. She also weaves yoga and mindfulness into her popular writing workshops and frequent appearances at writing conferences across the country.

She's the coauthor of *5-Minute Mindfulness*, as well as the bestselling *Plot Perfect, The Writer's Guide to Beginnings, Writing With Quiet Hands* and *Fixing Freddie: A True Story About a Boy, a Mom, and a Very, Very Bad Beagle*. She's also the author of *A Borrowing of Bones*, the first in a new mystery series from Minotaur Books. She was inspired to write *A Borrowing of Bones* by the hero working dogs she met through Mission K9 Rescue, and her own Newfoundland retriever mix rescue, Bear.

She began her career as a journalist and along the way added editor, acquisitions specialist, digital content manager and publishing executive to her repertoire, working for such media giants as WGBH, Disney, Gannett, F+W Media and Quayside. In 2012, she joined Talcott Notch Literary Services as senior literary agent and content strategist. Her specialties include crime fiction, women's fiction, upmarket fiction, MG and crossover YA, high-concept SFF, and nonfiction. She lives in New England with her family, Bear, Freddie and a torbie tabby named Ursula.